7 ROLES

GREAT

LEADERS

DON'T

DELEGATE

7 ROLES GREAT LEADERS

DON'T DELEGATE

TOM GEHRING

`ISBN 978-1-7327992-0-2 (paperback)
ISBN 978-1-7327992-2-6 (ebook)
ISBN 978-1-7327992-1-9 (hardcover)

Published by Far Peaks Publishing
San Diego, California
www.farpeaksconsulting.com

For ordering information or special discounts for bulk purchases or customized editions, please contact Far Peaks Publishing, (619) 206-8282

Cover and Inteior Design and composition by The Book Designers, www.bookdesigners.com

Publishing Consulting by Karla Olson, BookStudio, www.bookstudiobooks.com

Printed in the United States of America

DEDICATION

This book is dedicated to the two Teds in my life:

To my son, Ted, for all you taught me.

To my father, Ted, for all you taught me.

TABLE OF CONTENTS

FOREWORD

Why did I write this book?

I've spent a lifetime following and leading. I've learned by following great leaders, and I've learned by watching horrible leaders. Each of those leaders, phenomenal or awful, taught me something more about the art and science of leading.

I wrote this book because I believe one of the most important things we humans do is to teach the next generation—and teach them well. My purpose is to share the genius of the great leaders and to help you avoid the pitfalls of the horrid ones.

The acts of writing this book, of teaching leadership, and of raising a child have crystallized four decades of implicit or intuitive leadership concepts into something tangible that I can pass on to the next generation. It has been a joy to reflect on my past and to help my readers with their future.

I dedicated this book to my son, Ted, because it is by teaching that we learn, and to my father, Ted, because he silently taught so much by example.

I am neither an academic nor a theoretician. I am a pragmatic practitioner of getting stuff done. I hope you will forgive the lack of intellectual purity—but, this stuff works!

On a bitterly cold winter night almost 40 years ago, I was freezing and drenched in the cockpit on my first submarine, *USS Nautilus* (SSN 571). The cockpit of a submarine is a very small open space at the top of the conning tower only 25 feet above the waterline. We were returning to New London, Connecticut, after a month operating in the far reaches of the North Atlantic. Since I was the most recently qualified and most junior watch officer, I was naturally assigned the watch from midnight to dawn in a howling snowstorm. The enlisted lookout/phone talker and I were exposed to huge waves that routinely topped the cockpit, in visibility that varied from poor to zero.

That was the night I first understood leadership. And many years later, I understood and valued the importance of great leadership teachers.

With almost everyone onboard fast asleep, I was responsible for the safety of 120 lives and a billion-dollar nuclear submarine. I had to make decisions. I had to make difficult decisions. I had to make the right decisions. I had to make them promptly. It was thrilling. It was terrifying. It was leadership.

But I was ready. I had been well prepared by my seniors—who had spent many, many hours teaching, sharing, and inculcating their wisdom and experience.

I hope this book—like my seniors on *Nautilus* and my many teachers since—will give you the tools you need, so that you are ready when you are (figuratively) alone, cold, wet, and in the dark—and in charge.

Leadership will always be thrilling and terrifying. I hope you will have been taught well—and that this book makes a difference to you.

—Tom Gehring
San Diego, Summer 2018

INTRODUCTION AND ORGANIZATION

You are the leader. You are in charge (of something). **What exactly do you delegate?** Everything? Nothing? What?

Another way of asking the same question is **"What is my job, really?"**

I answer that first foundational question by identifying seven roles that you should not, or cannot, delegate. These are the **roles or responsibilities that only the leader can or should own— the seven non-delegables of leadership.**

Once you know what you cannot delegate, everything else can and should be appropriately and thoughtfully delegated!

Then I will answer the second foundational question: **How exactly does the leader successfully fulfill each of those seven non-delegable leadership roles?**

Section one will explain in three chapters what should not be delegated, and why. I will discuss my leadership paradigm in general terms, including how the roles of the leader

> Once you know what you cannot delegate, everything else can and should be appropriately and thoughtfully delegated!

and the team interact, the common pitfalls in implementing the paradigm, why this paradigm is applicable across the spectrum of leadership responsibilities, and the importance of a proactive mindset.

In section two, I will describe in detail the seven non-delegable roles.

Finally, in section three, I will present four case studies that will bring context and provide implementation insights into the seven non-delegable roles of the leader.

1

SECTION 1

THE PARADIGM

The Seven Non-Delegables

But first, what exactly is a paradigm?

A paradigm is a standard, a pattern, a set of ideas. A paradigm is a way of looking at something.

Start with the end in mind

Peter MacCracken, a San Diego communications wizard, reminded me of that age-old dictum for presenters: give your audience the punchline, explain how you got to the punchline, and close by reiterating the punchline.

So I will start in the first chapter by naming and sequencing the seven non-delegables.

> Every effective leader, sooner or later, will and must ask herself, *"What's my job, really?"* Stating the question just a little differently, *"What should I not delegate? What can I not delegate?"*

A paradigm for leadership

Every effective leader, sooner or later, will and must ask herself, *"What's my job, really?"*

Stating the question just a little differently: *"What should I not delegate? What can I not delegate?"*

In today's intellectually noisy and insatiably busy world, it's easy to not listen to yourself asking that most fundamental question.

The seven non-delegable roles and outcomes

I believe that any leader has seven non-delegable roles. Associated with each of those roles are specific outcomes. The roles and outcomes are listed in a logical, but not necessarily sequential, order.

With one exception, each of the roles is described by one word – a verb.

Sensing

The leader gathers, from many disparate internal and external sources, the data necessary to create a mental model of her organization in the environment in which that organization will operate.

The outcome of sensing is a clear strategic picture of today's reality.

Visioning

From that strategic picture of the present, the leader creates a vision for the future, and from that vision, she creates the attendant strategies to drive systemic change and achieve the vision.

The outcome of visioning is a path to a desirable future.

Acculturation

The leader sets and owns the culture of her organization.

The outcome of acculturation is the organizational and individual behaviors necessary to achieve the vision.

Enabling

The leader enables her followers by providing all the tools, tangible and intangible, necessary to implement the vision.

The outcome of enabling is followers who can achieve the vision.

Deciding

The leader makes the right decisions in the right way in the right time frame.

The outcome(s) of deciding are decisions that achieve the vision and are consistent with the culture.

Embracing responsibility

The leader embraces responsibility for everything that happens in her organization.

The outcome of embracing responsibility is ownership.

Mentoring

The leader selects, trains, and mentors the next generation of leaders.

The outcome of mentoring is a next generation that can pick up the baton of leadership and continue toward the vision in the absence of the current leadership.

It's a cycle that repeats itself

The seven non-delegable roles are related in a circular, not linear, progression.

In general, the cycle starts with sensing, then visioning, proceeds to acculturation, then enabling, then making decisions based on the vision, then taking responsibility for those decisions, and then creating the next generation.

And then you start over.

Because the world changes rapidly, the leader cannot simply follow the cycle once and declare victory.

It is highly likely that at some point in the future your strategic picture will change, and therefore a new vision and strategies are needed, and perhaps a new culture is required—and new tools. And the way you make decisions and to whom you delegate authority may change.

There is no such thing as "one-and-done" in leadership.

Some roles can, and frequently should, occur simultaneously

While I present the roles in a specific order, that sequence is not absolute.

While sensing must occur before visioning, and visioning precedes enabling and acculturation, the leader will be accepting responsibility, mentoring, and deciding continuously.

You do not have to wait for acculturation to complete before making good decisions, accepting responsibility, and mentoring.

An example of the circular and non-linear sequence of the seven non-delegables

Looking back on my 14-year stint as the CEO of the San Diego County Medical Society (SDCMS), there were (in hindsight) four very discrete strategic phases. Each phase was built on the challenges and successes of the previous phase, but each phase required a distinctly different approach. So the cycle of sensing – visioning – acculturation – enabling – deciding – taking responsibility – mentoring repeated itself four times.

In phase one, the focus was on survival. Not long after assuming the role of CEO, I sensed that SDCMS was fiscally unsustainable and that the culture was not aligned with the current generation of medical practice. Absent rapid corrective action, the future was bleak. Sensing resulted in a vision and a strategic plan to regain our financial footing and create a new culture. That drove changes in people, machines, and processes, with the attendant need for resources. All the while, I was deciding, taking responsibility, and mentoring.

But after several years, I sensed that while we were no longer in the organizational ICU, survival was not enough—we needed growth. My sense of low or no growth caused us to create a new vision, which engendered new strategies, which required new tools to enable our team. And we had to change the culture once again to emphasize growth, not just survival. All the while, I was mentoring, taking responsibility, and deciding.

And the cycle repeated itself twice more.

What is usually explicit about leadership roles?

Over the past decade, I have asked many leaders what roles, what functions, what portfolios, belong only to the leader, whether as CEO, as a C-suite resident, or as a workgroup leader.

Everyone responds with some variation on making decisions.

The topic of vision and strategies almost always comes up.

Hiring of senior staff and controlling/managing money are usually discussed as being the sole purview of the leader.

Taking responsibility comes up less frequently, but almost always with leaders who have military, medical or very senior leadership experience.

What is usually implicit about leadership roles?

What is surprising is what many highly effective leaders omit from the list of non-delegable leadership roles.

It's not because they don't know or accept these roles; it's that the unmentioned roles are implicit and therefore not in their forebrain.

The first goal of this book is making the non-delegable principal roles of the leader explicit, organized, and connected.

Almost no one I've asked has ever articulated that sensing is a leadership responsibility.

When I suggest that enabling, acculturation, accepting responsibility, and mentoring might also be roles for the CEO, very few disagree and most have an "aha" moment.

It is not that people don't appreciate the importance of sensing, enabling, acculturation, accepting responsibility, and mentoring. Rather it is that those roles are implicit, and therefore not afforded much explicit attention.

Experience has taught all of us that that which is not made explicit often does not happen. Not because it's unimportant, but because more "important" explicit tasks or roles push implicit roles to the sidelines.

Category 2 – Not urgent but important

Stephen Covey in his seminal book *First Things First* divides tasks or roles along two axes: important versus not important, and urgent versus not urgent.

He defines category 1 as urgent and important—in the firefighting analogy, putting out the fire.

Category 3 is urgent but not important. Regretfully, much of our day is spent in category 3. Emails, phone calls, office calls, and the list goes on and on.

Category 4, not urgent and not important, constitutes the many distractions of this attention-deficit-disorder-inducing world.

It's category 2, not urgent but important, where Covey recommends we spend our most valuable time. This would be analogous to fire prevention.

In this book, I am speaking to those tasks that belong to category 2. But more specifically, I want to give leaders a framework, a theory, a paradigm for those "not urgent yet important" roles that only belong to the leader.

The second goal of this book is giving leaders at all levels the tools they need to properly execute those roles that only belong to them—the non-delegables.

CHAPTER SUMMARY

- Every leader must continuously ask, "What's my job, really?"
- There are, in my model, seven non-delegables that define the role of the leader:
  - ✓ Sensing
  - ✓ Visioning
  - ✓ Acculturation
  - ✓ Enabling
  - ✓ Deciding
  - ✓ Embracing responsibility
  - ✓ Mentoring
- Every leader must continuously ask, "How exactly do I successfully fulfill each of those seven non-delegable leadership roles?"
- The seven roles are neither simultaneous nor perfectly sequential.
- The model is continuous, and the emphasis on each role is situational and overlapping.
- In general, sensing precedes visioning, visioning precedes acculturation and enabling, and deciding/embracing responsibility/ mentoring occur at any time during the leadership life cycle.
- There are two fundamental purposes for this book:
  - ✓ To make the non-delegables, the principal roles of the leader, explicit and connected.
  - ✓ To give leaders at all levels the tools they need to properly execute those roles that only belong to them— the non-delegables.

Setting the Context for the Seven Non-Delegables Paradigm

Why do I need a leadership paradigm?

There are some who are so gifted that leadership comes to them without any effort. For the rest of us, leadership is an art and science that is learned and developed over many years.

As an engineer, I believe that process rules. There is a

Paradigm, then process.

process for almost anything. And central to understanding, building, and modifying processes is a fundamental understanding of the underlying paradigm, model or theory.

Without that underlying paradigm, model or theory, a mastery of process gets you nowhere. Paradigm, then process.

As a young person, I was fascinated by electronic circuits in general, and transistors in particular. I chose Rice University because of its strong electrical engineering programs, thinking I was going to learn transistor circuit design.

The gateway course for electrical engineers at Rice was EE 343, *Transistor Circuit Design,* taught by Dr. C. Sidney Burrus. I will never forget the first day of class, as a group of very talented engineers-in-training was completely befuddled when Dr. Burrus told us that you could teach almost anyone transistor circuit design, but he wasn't going to do that! Instead, he was going to teach us the principles and theories and underlying mathematical models of transistors. Once we knew the principles and theory and mathematics, we could adapt them to almost any design situation. First theory/paradigm, then process. A lifelong lesson learned early!

> **Everyone needs a paradigm of leadership.**

Likewise, with leadership—almost anyone can learn the outward manifestations, the techniques, the processes of leadership. But to be a truly effective leader, you need to understand, absorb, and articulate an underlying model or theory of how you will lead.

And that's why everyone needs a paradigm of leadership.

But what is leadership?

If we need a paradigm for leadership, we'd better have a definition of leadership.

There are as many definitions of leadership as there are leaders, but I think it important to this book that I articulate my definition.

> **Leadership is taking a group of people to a place they would not have gotten to without you.**

Leadership is taking a group of people to a place they would not have gotten to without you.

Congratulations! What do I do now?

After years, perhaps even decades, of hard work and learning and climbing, you've achieved your goal—you're now the leader. You have the corner office! You get the big chair! You get to sit at the head of the table!

After the euphoria and the parties and the backslapping, at some point—hopefully soon after taking over, and ideally before assuming the title—you're going to sit in your corner office in your big chair and ask yourself, "What the heck am I really supposed to be doing as the leader? Should I really be doing whatever I'm doing now?"

Those to whom you report, unless they are particularly enlightened, assume you know both the right questions to ask and the right answers—after all, you are the boss and they just promoted you.

Those who report to you assume that you know the right answers because, after all, you are the boss.

And if you are the leader, and if for some reason you haven't thought deeply about those questions, no matter how small or large the organization, I hope that this book will stimulate you to ask—and answer—this most difficult and foundational question.

That the question is foundational is obvious.

What makes it so difficult is that there is no one right answer. Regretfully, there are no stone tablets to consult.

Allocating your two most precious resources

How do you allocate your two most important resources—your time and your attention—in a logical and organized manner?

If you don't have a paradigm of how to spend your time and focus, you will be at the whims of everyone else, and you will do whatever is loudest or closest or easiest or most appealing.

What any leader discovers very quickly is that his Day-Timer (for the Baby Boomers) or his Outlook or iPhone (for Gen X or the Millennials) is oversubscribed.

Everyone wants a piece of the boss's time. And the bad news is that this overloading likely will never change—there will always be many, many more demands on the leader's time than there are hours in the day.

> **If you don't have a paradigm of how to spend your time and focus, you will be at the whims of everyone else, and you will do whatever is loudest or closest or or easiest or most appealing.**

More importantly, the people asking for your time may not have the fundamental interests of the leader or the organization in mind. They usually have good intentions, but when they ask for an appointment, they are trying to solve something that's important to them. Said differently, everyone wants you to do what's important to them. That's why it's so important that you filter the demands on your time against what really matters. And what really matters must be driven by your leadership paradigm.

And it's not just your schedule and your time that are oversubscribed. While there are certainly exceptions, most among us have the capability for only a finite amount of focused and creative analytical thinking. At the end of an exhausting day (or week or month) filled with all-consuming meetings and crises and travel and email and phone calls, the probability that you will be able to come up with innovative and insightful thoughts is pretty low.

> **It's so important that you filter the demands on your time against what really matters. And what really matters must be driven by your leadership paradigm.**

Your bandwidth for the kind of deep thinking that leadership demands is limited, and therefore it is your responsibility to allocate it wisely. And you allocate your attention based on your leadership paradigm.

The first right question to ask

After many years of leadership and followership in the US Navy, and, after retirement from naval service and several years as a consultant with Booz|Allen|Hamilton, I was overjoyed to be asked to become CEO of a not-for-profit membership organization, the aforementioned SDCMS. The society represented over 8,000 doctors from many diverse healthcare systems in the eighth-largest city in the United States. In addition to being a professional challenge, it was also important to me personally— my wife, Cathy, is a physician who has always been involved in organized medicine. In fact, it was through her connections that I became interested in serving SDCMS. We would joke that I was working for her both at home and at the office!

After about three or four months as a newly minted CEO, I started asking myself during my daily lunchtime jog, *"What am I really supposed to be doing?"* Sure, there were fires to fight, meetings to attend, emails aplenty, speeches to give, and so many people to talk to, but deep in my thinking was a fundamental emptiness. Yes, I could make the trains run on time. Yes, I could prevent derailments. Yes, we could make the railroad not lose money.

But, continuing with the metaphor, were the trains going to the right places? Was train travel the optimal mode of transportation? What opportunities were we missing because we were thinking only about trains?

And the more I thought about these executional questions, the more I started to ask myself the foundational question: What, fundamentally, was I supposed to be doing as the boss?

And while many people were willing and able to provide executional answers and advice, no one helped me think through the foundational question.

"What am I really supposed to be doing as the CEO?"

Over the next years, I built a paradigm that answered the question "What am I really supposed to be doing as the CEO?"

But wait, there's a second and more important question!

Later, I realized that that the question of what you're supposed to be doing is a good one, but it is the penultimate question. The final question to ask and answer is "Why am I doing that which I am really supposed to be doing?"

This book is about answering those two fundamental and foundational questions. It is about managing the fundamental "why's."

"Why am I doing that which I am really supposed to be doing?"

We do best what we did last

In many, if not most, organizations, promotions are based on organizational or technical competence, combined with our superiors' belief (often, an educated guess) that the person being promoted will do well on the next rung on the ladder.

Even for organizations that have superlative leadership training and development programs, past performance is still not a guarantee of future success.

In their new role, first-time leaders or leaders with increased spans of control can easily revert to their proven technical or organizational competence. They are comfortable doing what they did on the last step of the ladder but uncomfortable or inexperienced on the current rung. As is often said, what got you here won't get you there.

Getting out of your prior comfort zone is easy to say and hard to do, particularly for newly minted leaders. But you have to become comfortable with asking and answering foundational and fundamental "why" questions about your new or expanded roles.

This book is all about defining the fundamental and foundational roles of leadership.

What's really new here?

The seven non-delegable roles are neither novel nor unexplored. Each of them has received a great deal of attention and documentation. Individually, I understood them and was implementing parts of most of them.

What's new, and the genesis of this book, is defining certain roles as not delegable, as well as defining their interrelationship and sequencing.

Why is that which is not delegable so important?

The conventional wisdom is to delegate as much as possible.

But if you first articulate those roles that the leader cannot or should not delegate, then you have defined the leader's unique roles.

In 2017, the Chief of Naval Operations, Admiral John Richardson, provided the following guidance to his senior leaders in a widely circulated letter:

> *"We need our leaders to spend more time thinking strategically and operationally. Too often we work tactically... It is expected that Navy senior leaders will carve out time in their schedules to think strategically and to radically delegate the tactical. We should identify 10–15 things to stop doing. Remove to the greatest extent possible your 'drag chutes.'"*

It's for leaders at every level of the organization—not just CEOs
It matters not whether you are a CEO of a large or small corporation, whether you are a divisional VP, whether you are the head of a small workgroup, or whether you run a family farm with two employees. The fundamental questions I have posited, and their answers, are the same.

What is this book not about?
While it is important to understand what the book is about, it is just as important to understand what it is not about.

There are a multitude of theories and books about almost every element of each of the seven non-delegables.

My goal is not to focus on technique, but rather to create a holistic view of how, and on what, leaders should spend those two incredibly precious resources: their time and their attention.

But what about my boss?
Everyone has a boss. That may be a person or an organization or a board or a constituency.

Communicating with your boss and maintaining relationships with your boss are clearly not delegable. I do not create a separate category of non-delegable for "leading up" because I believe that leading up is an amalgam of all the tools you use for leadership. In chapter 14, I give an explicit example of how the principles of the seven non-delegables can be applied to a situation where "leading up" is required. The remaining three examples in chapters 11 through 13 discuss various aspects of "leading up."

But what about the customer?

I am focused on what the leader does, but not *directly* on what the organization does for the customer. That I hardly talk about the customer in this book is a conscious decision but is not meant in any way to minimize the importance, the *raison d'être*, of the customer for the organization.

In fact, in figure 1 below, all that we are talking about—people, processes, strategies, and vision—center on the customer.

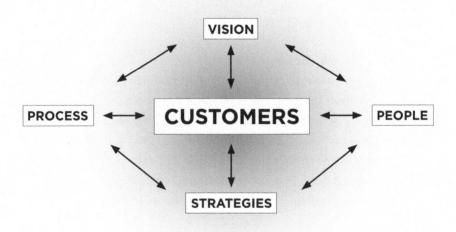

Figure 1

The people must be aligned with the processes, and the strategies must be aligned with the vision. But, in the final analysis, it's all about the customer—so the graphic in figure 1 helps me stay focused.

Chapter Contents

For each chapter, I will summarize the key takeaways, propose some concrete steps in the format of "What am I going to do differently on Monday morning?" and include (for each of the seven non-delegables) a one-page cartoon/graphic of what is involved in that non-delegable.

Common Terminology

Given the broad spectrum of leadership—from CEO of a large organization to a VP or department leader to overseeing a workgroup to running a small family business—I will use the word "leader" to represent anyone in any of those roles who has a leadership role.

CHAPTER SUMMARY

- I define leadership as taking a group of people to a place they would not have gotten to without you.
- The two most critical self-questions for the leader are:
    - ✓ What am I really supposed to be doing?
    - ✓ Why am I doing that which I am really supposed to be doing?
- Before focusing on the process of leadership (the "how"), you need to have an effective paradigm, theory or model of leadership (the "why"). Paradigm, then process.
- You allocate your two most important resources—time and attention—by using this (or any) leadership paradigm.
- By defining what you do not delegate, you have a blueprint for delegating everything else and focusing on what only you, the leader, should or can do.
- What is new about this book is defining certain roles as not delegable, as well as their interrelationship and sequencing.
- This book is not just for CEOs, but for every leader with one or more followers.

What Could Possibly Go Wrong?

Now that I've described the seven elements of my leadership paradigm—the non-delegable roles of the leader—let's do a pre-mortem to see what could possibly go wrong.

What's a pre-mortem?

Everyone is familiar with a post-mortem. When things go wrong, this is where the fingers are pointed, the voices are raised, the blame is assigned (usually to the innocent), etc. ...

The concept of a pre-mortem was developed to brainstorm anything and everything that could possibly go wrong before failure and to take proactive steps to preclude failure.[1]

The four "buts"

Using the philosophy of the pre-mortem, I identified the four most likely points of failure for implementing the seven non-delegables leadership paradigm.

And in the spirit of the pre-mortem, I also identified things you can do to prevent those points of failure.

---

1. The Pre-Mortem: A Simple Technique To Save Any Project From Failure, https://www.riskology.com/pre-mortem-technique/

But my schedule is full!

No one has complete control of their schedule and their commitments.

The more senior you are, the more you have control. Paradoxically, as you gain in seniority, the more commitments you have. While you may be able to choose some of your obligations, there are many time-consuming events that you simply cannot turn down.

The more junior you are, the less you perceive that you have control of your schedule, while paradoxically, the fewer external responsibilities you have.

Critical to becoming an effective leader is that you wrest as much control of your schedule and your commitments from those who wish to fill it up. You must be proactive, not reactive. You must fence time on your schedule to engage in the non-delegable roles. You must take time for the important but not urgent matters described by Covey.

> **You must fence time on your schedule to engage in the non-delegable roles.**

If you schedule yourself, this becomes a matter of self-discipline.

If you have a scheduler or an executive assistant, it's about convincing—or directing—that person to make sure that there is plenty of time on your calendar for the non-delegable roles.

But I don't want to delegate that...

The Venn diagram of figure 2 easily explains where you need to focus.

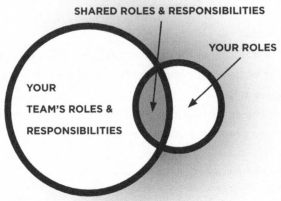

SHARED ROLES & RESPONSIBILITIES

YOUR ROLES

YOUR TEAM'S ROLES & RESPONSIBILITIES

Figure 2

Your team has either technical or organizational roles that are not in the leader's purview. In a large organization, it would be ludicrous to have the leader managing accounts receivable. However, for smaller organizations, it becomes much easier for the leader to step into roles for which she is technically qualified. A small family enterprise may very well have the leader doing accounts receivable. The smaller the organization, the more important for the leader to be very selective about accepting roles that are the purview of her subordinates.

Likewise, there are roles that by statute, convention, or direction are outside the scope of your team member's skills or authorization. For example, in a large organization, signing the annual report to shareholders is legally the role of the leader.

The difficulty arises in those roles on the Venn diagram that are shared—where it is realistic and possible for either the team or the leader to be executing those roles.

If the leader has a unique skill or strength, then she may get involved in a shared area. However, it is incumbent on the leader to groom someone on the team to assume principal responsibility for that role.

If the leader has a strong interest or passion in a specific role, then she has to make an explicit choice. Is this interest or passion consistent with the vision of the organization, or is it tangential? If it is part of the vision, then it may not be a shared role and responsibility. If it is not coincident with the vision, then it's a hobby, and the leader needs to drop that role.

> **The leader needs to minimize any role that could be accomplished by the team, and therefore the shared role part of the Venn diagram should be as small as possible.**

In general, the leader needs to minimize any role that could be accomplished by the team, and therefore the shared role part of the Venn diagram should be as small as possible.

But I'm not the CEO...

The most common refrain I hear is *"while your theories are all good and wonderful, the reality is that I'm not the CEO, I'm just a department head and not someone who is in charge of the entire organization."*

> **Teddy Roosevelt famously said, *"Do what you can, where you're at, with what you have."***

Teddy Roosevelt famously said, *"Do what you can, where you're at, with what you have."*

If you are not the CEO, you do not have as much control as if you were. But you do have *some* control. If you have a leadership role, you have control. You are helpless only if you choose to be.

And sometimes, it is better to ask forgiveness than permission.

But my boss doesn't want to play...

The second most common concern voiced by leaders in the middle of an organization is *"my boss doesn't get it."*

Many books have been written about leading up—how to get your boss to sing the same tune that you're humming.

You must factor in the reality that a leader above you may not see the value in what you are doing. Without repeating the many words that have been written, the single most effective way to get your boss to sing along

> **If there is a tangible "what's in it for them," your boss will (usually) play!**

is to demonstrate concrete value from the initiatives associated with the seven non-delegables.

If there is a tangible "what's in it for them," your boss will (usually) play!

I devote an entire case study, chapter 14, to the issues and nuances associated with getting your boss (and sometimes your peers) onboard.

CHAPTER SUMMARY

- Ask beforehand what could go wrong with implementing the seven non-delegables leadership paradigm in your specific reality.
- The four most common points of failure for the paradigm are:
  - ✓ I don't have the time for my non-delegable roles.
  - ✓ I don't want to delegate that.
  - ✓ I'm powerless because I'm not the Big Boss.
  - ✓ I'm powerless because my boss doesn't want to play.
- Fence time on your schedule to engage in the non-delegable roles.
- Minimize any role that could be accomplished by your team.
- You are only powerless if you choose to be.

WHAT AM I GOING TO DO DIFFERENTLY ON MONDAY?

- I am going to aggressively take charge of my schedule and eliminate those items that are not critical to leadership.
- I am going to constantly ask myself whether tasks are associated with shared or delegable roles, and then reduce or eliminate those tasks.
- I am going to take charge where I can, and not become a powerless follower.
- I am going to find at least one specific "what's in it for my boss."

2

SECTION 2

THE SEVEN
NON-DELEGABLES

SENSING

Sensing

The leader gathers, from many disparate internal and external sources, the data necessary to create a mental model of the organization in the environment in which that organization operates.

The leader is the Chief Sensor.

Why is this the longest chapter?

As I was obtaining feedback on my initial drafts, many reviewers commented on the disproportionate length of this chapter.

As a leadership process, sensing is the least documented of the seven non-delegables, and yet is the most intellectually challenging. There are few, if any, roadmaps to sensing, so most of this chapter presents material I have not been able to find elsewhere.

Data to information to strategic picture

I love the picture in figure 3 because it captures what the leader is doing every day.

Figure 3

Leaders are absorbing data from tens, perhaps even hundreds, of sources every day. Over time, the leader as Chief Sensor turns that data into information, and information into a picture of the present reality.

> **Leaders are absorbing data from tens, perhaps even hundreds, of sources every day. Over time, the leader as Chief Sensor turns that data into information, and information into a picture of the present reality.**

There are three major steps in sensing: obtaining data, turning data into information, and turning information into a model.

Turning data into information is hard enough, but the real work of leadership is turning information into a strategic picture of how the organization fundamentally functions in the environment it occupies.

Look at many data sources

It is critical to look for data from many sources, so that the generated information is reliable and actionable. Any one data point, or even multiple data points, can be erroneous or misleading. Having multiple sources allows data to be confirmed or discarded.

The leader must assess, both for individual data points and in general for a given data source, the accuracy and believability of the source and the data.

Here's an example from my Navy days. The submarine force developed a technique called the Contact Evaluation Plot (CEP). If we were looking for a target while at periscope depth, the submarine would receive information from a number of sources—multiple acoustic sonar signals, visual information from the periscope, radio and radar data, and external cueing (intelligence). In addition to the actual data, we had a pretty good idea of the general accuracy of the data source.

Data fusion

How did we determine where the target really was? The answer was data fusion.

While the technology to implement the CEP has improved from a human with a large piece of paper to an electronic gizmo that automatically plots information on a big screen, the principle has not changed. Get every scrap of data into a single place—the CEP, then factor in the reliability and accuracy of the data, and then make an educated guess.

Figure 4 is a simplistic representation of data fusion. For this example, squares are sonar signals, X's are electronic data, plus signs are visual info, and triangles and stars represent external cueing.

The line represents the best estimate of what the target is doing. While the line does not necessarily align perfectly with any one piece of data, it is the interpolation of all the data, the best-estimate one-line fit through the multiple data points, that is the strength of the data fusion.

> While the line does not necessarily align perfectly with any one piece of data, it is the interpolation of all the data, the best-estimate one-line fit through the multiple data points, that is the strength of the data fusion.

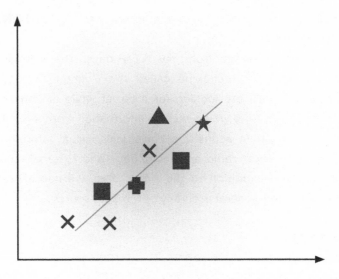

Figure 4

Likewise, as the leader of something other than a submarine conducting targeting, you must intake multiple data points with variable accuracy and fuse them into a picture of the truth.

Conflicting, misleading, or incomplete data
Leaders are faced every day with conflicting, misleading, or incomplete data.

When the data is inconclusive, the leader is wise to avoid drawing immediate conclusions. Time is your friend.

The leader can create reliable information in the face of divergent or inconsistent data by waiting until multiple sources and multiple data points converge.

Going back to our CEP example, in figure 5 you can see that the triangles and stars, representing external target cueing to the submarine, are telling a different story than the organic assets—sonar, radio/radar, and visual. The wise submariner waits, gathers additional data, and then integrates all the information to obtain more reliable targeting.

When I was the newly minted chief operating officer (COO)

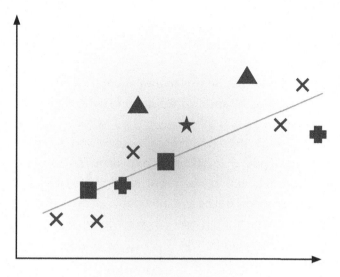

Figure 5

of a large industrial organization, one of my department heads, let's call him Jeff, immediately became a management challenge. Jeff was older than his peers with a crusty personality. He had incredible experience and was widely respected for his professional skill. But I quickly started receiving reports of problematic interactions between Jeff and his peers. Interestingly, there were no reports of problems between Jeff and his customers. I was faced with conflicting and likely incomplete data. What to do?

So I gathered more data. I looked to different sources—by talking to people other than the complainers. I investigated the specifics of the data. I spoke to Jeff's customers and other outsiders who knew him. Eventually, I developed a more robust picture of Jeff—I turned more data into better information. And I was able to intervene appropriately and effectively.

> **I did not wait until I had perfect information from infinite data, but I also did not jump to conclusions from early and isolated data. Balancing speed and accuracy is the perpetual challenge of sensing.**

I did not wait until I had perfect information from infinite data, but I also did not jump to conclusions from early and isolated data. Balancing speed and accuracy is the perpetual challenge of sensing.

From data to information to a mental model

The first two steps in sensing are gathering data and turning data into information.

The final step in the sensing process is to convert the information into a mental model that articulates a fundamental understanding of the inputs, outputs, and inner workings of the organization.

The mental model can be any combination of detail and formality.

While the format of a model is not important, what is critical is that the leader can articulate the model in writing. It is the discipline of forcing yourself to put the model on paper—and then critiquing and evolving the model until you are satisfied with it—that will lead you to accuracy.

> No matter how large or complex an organization, the leader must be able to reduce the size and complexity to something that is easy to understand.

Simplicity matters. No matter how large or complex an organization, the leader must be able to reduce the size and complexity to something that is easy to understand. And that's damnably difficult. Which is why it usually takes time to develop the model.

Okay, so what does this model you keep talking about look like?

There are limitless ways of modeling an organization. There is no one right answer. There is no professor to give you a grade on the model. But, if you can explain to yourself and others how the organization functions at a macroscopic level, then you have an effective model!

After several years at SDCMS, I developed a single-page graphic to explain what the organization was about and how it worked, see figure 6.

The interrelationship of the major functions on a single sheet of paper was incredibly helpful to understand the organization and allowed me to pinpoint where the organization needed to improve.

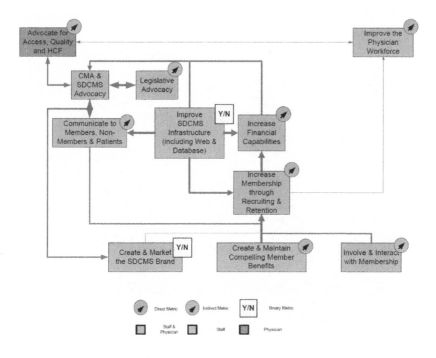

Figure 6 - The SDCMS Mental Model

Using the model, I could quickly and effectively explain the organization to complete strangers. I used the mental model to create an elevator message[2] for SDCMS.

During healthcare reform in 2010, a one-page model of the proposed healthcare financing system was developed by a member of Congress, displayed as figure 7. The principal takeaway, obvious to any junior high student, was that the system was inordinately complex and could not be improved without wholesale strategic changes.

The model is the strategic picture

Another way to think about the model is as a strategic picture.

---

2. An elevator message is a clear, brief message or "commercial" about your organization. It's typically about 30 seconds long, the time it takes people to ride from the top to the bottom of a building in an elevator.

It's strategic because it looks at the entire organization in the context of the environment in which it exists.

It's a picture because looking at it creates rapid understanding.

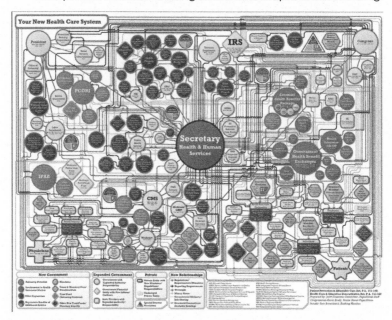

Figure 7 - Rep. Kevin Brady's representation of the of the post ACA Healthcare System

And thinking about it as a strategic picture allows one to segue directly into the leader's second non-delegable role: visioning.

Look at the context of the model

Nothing operates in a vacuum. Having a fundamental understanding of the environment may be an obvious prerequisite for an accurate model, but it is amazing how many times a great model built in a environmental vacuum can lead an organization astray.

> A great model built in a environmental vacuum can lead an organization astray.

In 2001, the Medical Society had been around for more than 130 years. One look at the strategic picture, or mental model, I found on arrival told me that we were focused on a rapidly shrinking constituency. In the days following the managed care revolution, the solo or small-group-practice physician—think of the character Dr. Marcus Welby of the eponymous TV show—was rapidly being overtaken by medium and large groups of physicians. Yet, our model was focused almost exclusively on the solo or small-group-practice physician.

The model that had worked for 130 years was rapidly becoming irrelevant because the environment had changed.

Why is sensing the first role in the circle of the seven non-delegables?

Before creating a vision for the future, one must start with a solid grounding in the present.

There are many examples of organizations that have launched well-designed visions and strategies based on a faulty understanding of the present organization and/or the current

> **It is so critical to sense first, *then* create a model, and only *then* start the process of visioning and strategizing.**

environment. The outcome of a great vision and strategy based on a faulty model is predictable and usually not pleasant.

The oft repeated example of a great vision in the wrong environment is "becoming the world's best buggy whip manufacturer" in 1910.

That is why it is so critical to sense first, *then* create a model, and only *then* start the process of visioning and strategizing.

How long should this take?

Sensing will take longer than you think.

Creating an accurate mental model involves a great deal of data assimilation and information processing by the leader. It requires the leader to test the nascent mental model against current and often dynamic realities.

All of this data assimilation and processing takes time. Lots of time.

Counterintuitively, the more severe the problems facing the organization, the shorter the time it takes to create the model—particularly if the organization is broken or breaking.

When I took over the Pacific Fleet Process Improvement Team late in my Navy career, it took me about a week to develop the strategic picture. It was pretty easy—the team was dysfunctional, and the organization was perceived as useless.

> **Don't over-study the problem if the picture is already clear.**

So don't over-study the problem if the picture is already clear.

Why is this the leader's task?

The leader is the only person in the organization who has access to all the information within the organization. There is nothing that the leader cannot access, since no one can legally withhold information from the leader.

There is an important caveat to this unfettered access. The unfortunate reality is that the more senior you get, the more filters are applied to the information, and the higher the probability that the information is either inaccurate or misleading.

It is precisely because the leader, and often only the leader, can cut through the obfuscation, whether deliberate or inadvertent, that he is the Chief Sensor.

It is usually only the leader who has the context and the contacts to obtain relevant and important information from outside the organization. The ability of the leader to communicate with fellow leaders is a privilege not usually accorded to members of his team. The leader's ready access to seminars, colloquia, high-level meetings, and other information sources is unrivaled within the organization. It is precisely because of that access to his peers that being the Chief Sensor is the responsibility of the leader.

You can easily drown in data

While you have access to all the data, it does not mean you should receive all the data. It is very easy to become overwhelmed or distracted by excessive or irrelevant data.

I will never forget the first meeting I had with our chief financial officer as a newly minted CEO. I asked her to give me a financial snapshot of the organization, and I received a stack of paper three-quarters of an inch thick. Absolutely complete, and utterly useless. We evolved to a single sheet of paper that quickly gave me the key metrics, and we dug deeper if the metrics flagged a problem.

Shape the data you get routinely

As the leader, you have the privilege of making sure the dashboard you're looking at is exactly the way you want, so you can process the data and turn it into information.

You must shape the data that comes to you by clearly articulating how, what, and when data should come to you.

> You must shape the data that comes to you by clearly articulating how, what, and when data should come to you.

There are two benefits to an effective dashboard: it gets you the information you need, and the dashboard becomes a focusing tool for the organization. As has been said many times, what interests my boss fascinates me!

Is the data you're getting accurate?

Do not underestimate how often people will not be forthright and forthcoming with necessary data, particularly bad news. I do not mean to encourage cynicism, but a healthy skepticism about the data presented to you is an excellent trait. Looking for confirming data from a different source is an excellent way to avoid getting bamboozled. Another excellent technique for leaders is to ask probing questions about whether the data is accurate and/or relevant.

Having good instincts is vitally important to a leader. When data feels wrong, I cannot overemphasize the importance of following your instincts.

There is data (and information) in success and failure

Admiral Hyman Rickover, the founder of the nuclear-powered U.S. Navy, was known for mercilessly probing both success and failure, although he did focus more on failure than success, by repeatedly asking "why." He would continue to ask "why" until he got to the bedrock of causality. Once he understood the reasons something happened, he focused on the corrective action.

As a leader, anytime you see something out of the ordinary—be it success or failure—it is important to get to that fundamental truth of what caused the success or failure. Therein lies a tremendous amount of both data and information.

> **Anytime you see something out of the ordinary—be it success or failure—it is important to get to that fundamental truth of what caused the success or failure.**

Admiral Rickover was quoted as saying that the first five times he asked "why," the answer belonged to him, but the answer to the sixth "why" belonged to God. There is a plaque in my office that has "WHY?" engraved on it six times. It is there to remind myself to probe relentlessly until I truly understand, and yet at some point causality becomes a matter of faith.

My last at-sea command, the USS McKee, was a very large surface ship that served as a floating repair workshop for submarines. Captain Tom Etter, my skipper and a fellow submariner, and I were used to the rigorous standards of submarine nuclear propulsion. We insisted on the same cleanliness and maintenance standards for *McKee*'s conventional, non-nuclear propulsion plant—as well as for the rest of the ship! Why, the *McKee* engineers grumbled, were we so doggone obsessed with cleanliness? After all, *McKee* was not a nuclear submarine!

Captain Etter and I were conducting a routine walk-through of the engine room when we spotted very faint traces of oil and dirt on a previously immaculately painted piece of boiler insulation. Had we not insisted on extremely high standards of cleanliness and preservation, we would never have seen the slight discoloration. Had we not been walking through on a routine basis, we would not have spotted the anomaly. Had we not seen the anomaly, insisted on an investigation, and acted on the report, we would not have discovered (and repaired) a failing fastener on the boiler access cover.

A potentially catastrophic failure was averted by creating systems that highlighted anomalous behavior, and then insisting on getting to the root cause of anomalous behavior.

Lack of data can be information

One of the most difficult and nuanced things for a leader to do is to translate lack of data into information.

We are all trained to look for signals. We are not trained to look at the absence of signals as information.

When a model predicts certain data in the future, it is easy to see that something has changed when the actual data is different than was predicted. This is what looking for an inflection point is all about.

However, when a model predicts certain data in the future and no data arrives, its absence can easily be overlooked.

> If the leader understands the expected behavior of people or a model, then he should be particularly alert when an expected data point does not appear.

In Arthur Conan Doyle's short story "Silver Blaze," Sherlock Holmes cracks the case because a watchdog did not bark when the murderer passed very close to the ever-vigilant canine. Why, posed the great detective, would the dog have remained silent? The answer, obvious in hindsight, was that only the owner of the dog would not incite furious barking.

Understanding and using the metaphor of "the dog that didn't bark" is critical to the effective leader. If the leader understands the expected behavior of people or a model, then he should be particularly alert when an expected data point does not appear.

There are no fewer than two explanations when the expected does not happen.

The first, and easiest, interpretation is random or insignificant behavior. For example, the reason the boss didn't invite you to the big retreat is that he forgot.

The second, and more difficult, interpretation is that the absence of data is not simply a random event, but a sign of something deeper. Perhaps the reason you didn't get invited to the big retreat is that your job is no longer considered important.

In either case, it is the role of the leader to look for confirming or disconfirming data from alternative sources.

> **Being alert for lack of data is so important because change will often announce itself with silence.**

Being alert for lack of data is so important because change will often announce itself with silence.

Do I look at the forest or the trees?

There is a saying about not being able to see the forest for the trees. It means that the big picture is unclear because people are looking at the minutia. I think that metaphor is misleading.

The leader must be able to look at both the forest, the big picture, and some trees, some details. Thus, a sensing leader must do two ostensibly contradictory things almost simultaneously.

First, look at the micro. I believe the leader must look at the right trees in the forest. One must be able to delve down into the detail when and where appropriate. The key is to focus on the right part of the right trees at the right time. While experience is helpful here, over time the leader will develop the instinct as to which details matter and are relevant to the big picture.

The leader must be able to look at both the forest, the big picture, and some trees, some details.

Second, look at the macro. Seeing the big picture is so critical to the leader that it has almost become a caricature. For example, it is easy while sitting on a Brazilian beach to see only the horizon, while the big picture escapes. It is not obvious from your view of the horizon at sea level that South America and Africa were once the same continent. But from a satellite at 200 kilometers above the Earth, it is obvious.

Early in my career, I served on an older submarine where one of the most challenging and dangerous evolutions was loading and offloading torpedoes. These two-ton, 20-foot-long monsters were swung to and from the ship by a crane and lowered into the torpedo room by a complex system of hydraulics, tackle, ropes, and wires. For the early nuclear submarines, this Rube Goldberg system (later and current loading systems are much simpler, safer, and more efficient) demanded intense training and teamwork— it was not hard to screw up. As the Weapons Officer, I was responsible for the safety and efficiency of loading weapons.

So how to supervise this? After all, I had no physical function in bringing the torpedo on and off the ship, but I was responsible for everything.

I did three things to make sure that the job was successful. First, I became an expert on every aspect of the weapons move so that I knew exactly what to look for, when to look for it, and where to look for it. I knew the micro, cold.

Second, nothing was moved until I granted permission to do so—after satisfying myself that we were ready, and after I had received the captain's permission to proceed.

And third, I physically positioned myself far enough from the action to see the entire evolution—the literal big picture—while close enough to spot a potential problem. I had the macro and the micro perspectives, literally.

Once, from 50 feet away, at the end of a very long and exhausting day of moving weapons, I could see that the team operating the hydraulics used to lower the torpedo had wound the rope on the capstan head clockwise instead of counter-clockwise. Sounds trivial, but it wasn't, as the mistaken direction directly affected the efficacy of a safety system.

> **Standing back far enough to observe the big picture while simultaneously knowing what details to look at are hallmarks of an effective Chief Sensor.**

I was able to shortstop a potentially significant problem by knowing where to look, standing back far enough to see the big picture but close enough to spot a specific problem.

Standing back far enough to observe the big picture while simultaneously knowing what details to look at are hallmarks of an effective Chief Sensor.

Signal-to-noise—time is your friend

In many cases, it is not a lack of data but too much random data that creates a lack of clarity.

As an electrical engineer, I trained in signal processing, based on the signal being greater than noise. In the real world, there is a tremendous amount of literal and figurative noise. The trick as a leader is to extract the signal—to obtain the picture—from all the random noisy behavior.

In looking for the signal above the noise, the key is to wait until enough signal has built up so that it stands out from the noise. That means that one must be patient to wait for the data to converge on the information above the random behavior.

A great example of this principle at work is in the stock market. The long-term investor is well served to ignore short-term fluctuations or oscillations. Unless you are a day trader, you should base your decisions on monthly or yearly stock price trends—where random or short-term behavior is factored out.

The Chief Sensor in a subjective, not objective, world

Much of the data you will deal with is subjective and will defy easy numerical interpretation.

I fully appreciate the duality of data—it is both subjective and objective.

The principles that I lay out below—interpolation, extrapolation, looking for inflection points, and looking for missing or absent data—are as applicable to subjective data as they are to objective data. It's just that the graphs are prettier and it's easier to do the math for objective data!

A two-dimensional example of turning data into information

Math-o-phobes fear not—while the following discussion looks math intense, it's really the principles that matter.

Even the most basic organization lives in a multidimensional world. But, for the sake of pedagogical simplicity, let's assume you are the leader in a two-dimensional world. For the sake of the example, all the data relevant to your organization can be plotted in two dimensions, a classic X-Y graph.

For the purposes of our two-dimensional example, the *data* resides in the dots (or shapes), and the *information* resides in the straight line plotted through the dots (or shapes).

> ▶ **THE FIRST PRINCIPLE OF SENSING:** *All the relevant data must be ingested and processed.* In the two-dimensional example, it is easily plotted. In the complex real world, all the data is not necessarily plotted but rather absorbed and integrated into the leader's head.

Let's look at an example of how data in a two-dimensional world clarifies the picture over time.

Explaining the past and the present

In the initial left-hand plot of figure 8 below, a reasonable initial interpolation (information) is sketched through the dots (data). However, in the right-hand plot, as more dots (data) becomes available, an alternative interpolation (information) is possible and in fact, more believable.

► **THE SECOND PRINCIPLE OF SENSING:** *The more data you have, the more reliable your information and the more accurate your model.*

► **THE THIRD PRINCIPLE OF SENSING:** *There are multiple ways to interpolate and extrapolate from the data to create information.*

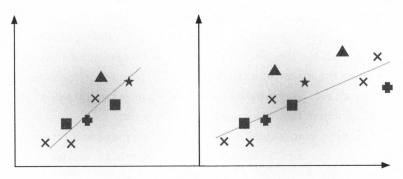

Figure 8

The left- and right-hand lines in figure 9 below are both reason-able interpolations of the same data.

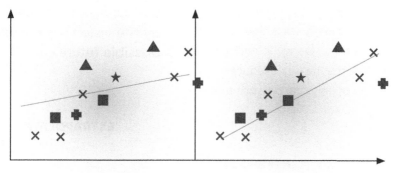

Figure 9

What does this mean for the leader? After some period, the leader will start to develop a model that fits the data. Early in the process, that model may be neither unique nor accurate. As time moves on, the fidelity of the model increases as more data converges on the model that fits the current data and explains what has happened to date.

Extrapolation, or predicting the future

Once the leader has built the model, the next step is to use that mental model to predict the future. Reverting to our two-dimensional example, one would extrapolate the relationship to some point in the future to predict a relationship between

You interpolate present and past. You extrapolate to the future.

the two variables. In figure 10 below, the dotted line represents predicted future behavior based on the past and present.

You interpolate present and past. You extrapolate to the future.

It is important to understand that an effective model must have some predictive capability to allow the leader to forecast a future.

A healthy skepticism on the part of the leader is important to ensure that he is not seduced by the vision of only one possible future.

A healthy skepticism on the part of the leader is important to ensure that he is not seduced by the vision of only one possible future.

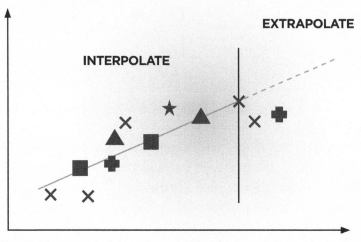

EXTRAPOLATE

INTERPOLATE

Figure 10

Inflection points, when prediction and reality diverge

The leader, the Chief Sensor, must be particularly alert if the data from the predicted future diverges from the data from the actual future.

In the first case the world didn't change, but our model needs to be more accurate. In the second case, the model was accurate up to a point, but then the world changed, and now the model needs to be fixed.

In our two-dimensional example in figure 11, the actual data points are starting to diverge from the predictions of the two-dimensional interpolation. There are two possibilities for this divergence:

First, the model was inaccurate and needs to be revised because additional data indicates an adjustment

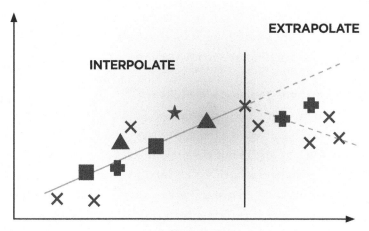

INTERPOLATE

EXTRAPOLATE

Figure 11

Often the leader is the first to recognize (or should be the first to recognize) an inflection point, and therefore that a systemic change is imminent or has already occurred.

to the model is required. This calls for incremental change.

Second, the model was accurate for the past, but something has changed, and a new model needs to be created. This calls for fundamental or strategic change.

The difference between the first and the second case above is critical. In the first case the world didn't change, but our model needs to be more accurate. In the second case, the model was accurate up to a point, but then the world changed, and now the model needs to be fixed.

If the model changed, is it incremental or fundamental change? Well, which is it—incremental change or fundamental change or no change?

The leader must wait until more data arrives, or look for confirming/contradicting additional data from other sources.

▶ **THE FOURTH PRINCIPLE OF SENSING:** *The leader must be constantly looking at the data for indications of systemic change.*

Often the leader is the first to recognize (or should be the first to recognize) an inflection point, and therefore that a systemic change is imminent or has already occurred.

Systemic change—The model is broken

Thomas Kuhn wrote *The Structure of Scientific Revolutions*, a seminal work that created a theory for how paradigms or models shift. But it is not just about scientific revolutions—it is a model for how the theory of a business can and will change.

When enough differences between the predicted and actual data occur, the existing model is thrown into a state of crisis. New models, perhaps ones previously discarded, are tested. A new model is formed, which gains its following. An intellectual battle takes place between the followers of the old and new models. A new model does not triumph by convincing its opponents and making them see the light, but rather because its opponents eventually die out while a new generation grows up that is familiar with it.

How is this part of the sensing process?

Paraphrasing the aforementioned Admiral Rickover, when something doesn't work, ask why until you get an answer that gets at the root cause, not the symptoms.

For a membership organization such as SDCMS, the fundamental metrics are membership count and total dues revenue. After seven years of steady, almost linear, growth, membership gradually plateaued and total revenue started to drop. No matter how hard we worked, we could not get our two strategic metrics to move in the right direction. In Kuhn's construct, the paradigm that SDCMS used to recruit and retain physicians had to change dramatically.

In fact, this failure of our two most important metrics to continue to improve was the first clue that we again needed to change our vision and strategies. This realization became the basis for the third distinct phase of SDCMS' strategic growth, with a new model, a new vision, new tools and a new culture.

Einstein's definition of insanity is doing the same thing over and over and expecting a different result. Kuhn said it more elegantly, but when you are figuratively beating your head against the wall because you cannot make the current model work, it's time to change paradigms.

> **When you are figuratively beating your head against the wall because you cannot make the current model work, it's time to change paradigms.**

Systemic change—The process/technology has changed

It is not just an underlying theory of the business—the paradigm—that can change. Technologies and processes that implement that model also change.

Clayton Christensen, in a seminal *Harvard Business Review* article "The Theory of Disruptive Technologies," created a model for knowing what to do when a disruptive technology arrives on the scene. Christensen's theory is just as applicable to processes as it is to technologies.

Christensen differentiates between sustaining innovation, with steady improvement and a focus on current customers, and disruptive innovation, where the technology and/or the processes associated with the business have completely and radically changed.

Christensen posits that sustaining innovation means listening to the current customers, making performance improvements required by the mainstream market, and steadily increasing the performance of the technology or processes.

At some point, a disruptive technology or process will appear. This radical shift sacrifices current performance, has a completely different attribute set, but is financially not yet attractive. The current customers are not interested.

As time moves on, the disruptive innovation surpasses the

sustaining innovation and creates a whole new class of customers. Old suppliers frantically try to catch up, but most old suppliers die or wither away.

A great example of a disruptive innovation is Christensen's discussion of floppy disks. When the first personal computers arrived on the scene, they contained 5.25" floppy disks for read/write storage. The manufacturers of the 5.25" floppy disks were making steady and significant improvement in the capability of the disks. Life was good. Then someone invented the 3.5" rigid disk. At inception, the performance of the 3.5" disk was inferior to the current technology, and both the manufacturers and users of the current technology were not interested. But two things changed their world. First, the 3.5" disk was improving in cost and storage performance much more rapidly than the 5.25" floppy disk—in nonmathematical terms, it was getting better faster. Second, the 3.5" disk was perfectly suited to something no one had ever seen before—a portable computer, a.k.a. the laptop. As a direct result, the 5.25" floppy disk manufacturers went out of business, and a whole new business was invented—the laptop.

I believe strongly in asking "why" until you get to the root cause of a specific issue. Recall my plaque with the six "WHYs" from a previous chapter. The leader should be particularly alert for new processes or technologies that everyone is pooh-poohing as simply not viable. First, determine whether the technology or the process is disruptive or sustaining. Then define the strategic significance of the

> **The leader should be particularly alert for new processes or technologies that everyone is pooh-poohing as simply not viable.**

disruptive technology—but don't ask your current customer.

A great example is healthcare, where today everyone is focused on the Baby Boomer generation and their challenges of aging. Yet, almost no one is talking to the new customer, the young.

How is this part of the sensing process?

The leader needs to be ever so alert for the symptoms of a technology or process that is about to change.

> ▶ **THE FIFTH PRINCIPLE OF SENSING:** *Once you identify an inflection point, you must decide which has to change—the model or the processes/systems/technologies that implement the model—or both!*

Change repeats

Just like Kuhn's theory of paradigm shifts, Christensen's theory of disruptive processes and technologies is repetitive and cyclic. Paradigm shifts or disruptive processes are not "one and done" behaviors.

In Christensen's seminal work, he cites the case of the data discs—the 8" floppy transitioning to the 5.25" floppy transitioning to the 3.5" rigid drive... And of course, today we have thumb drives, a.k.a. flash drives.

Change, like the weather, is rhythmic and never-ending.

What is the difference between Kuhn and Christensen?

While there are many interpretations, I believe Kuhn's paradigm shifts point to a fundamental change in the theory of the business, while Christensen points to a fundamental change in the processes/technologies of the business.

> Kuhn's paradigm shifts point to a fundamental change in the theory of the business, while Christensen points to a fundamental change in the processes/technologies of the business.

And, it is not hard to conceive of a situation where the two types of change are concurrent.

For example, the advent of the Electronic Medical Record, a change in the technology/process, is causing fundamental changes in the way medicine is being practiced.

So build the model, already!

There is no cookbook for sensing.

The reason it is a non-delegable role is because only the leader has access to all the information both within the organization and without.

After a certain amount of time, and there is no formula to tell you when it's time, the leader needs to start building a model of how the organization really works.

There are likely reams of detailed flow charts, graphs, and descriptions—and the larger the organization, the more detail there is. The weighty tomes of today are not useful to the leader, particularly if the organization is in crisis.

If you can't fit the model on a single sheet of paper, it's probably not useful for your thinking.

I will admit that for a large organization you may need to use a large sheet of paper. Nonetheless, the Chief Sensor proceeds from data to information to a model for the organization.

CHAPTER SUMMARY

- The leader gathers, from many disparate internal and external sources, the data necessary to create information to develop a mental model—a strategic picture—of the organization in the environment in which it operates.
- The process of sensing is a three-step process:
  - ✓ obtaining the data,
  - ✓ turning the data into information, and
  - ✓ turning the information into a mental model.
- The five principles of sensing:
  - ✓ All the relevant data must be ingested and processed.
  - ✓ The more data you have, the more reliable your information and your model.
  - ✓ There are multiple ways to interpolate and extrapolate from the data to create information.
  - ✓ The leader must be constantly looking at the data for inflection points—indications of systemic change.
  - ✓ Once you identify an inflection point, you must decide which has to change—the model or the processes/systems/ technologies that implement the model—or both!
- When obtaining the data:
  - ✓ The leader must patiently gather data from many sources, selected and shaped for easy understanding and analysis.
  - ✓ Data comes from macro and selected micro perspectives.
  - ✓ The leader must be ever alert for the absence of expected data.
- When turning the data into information:
  - ✓ Turning data into information is complex and time-consuming.
  - ✓ To create information from data, the leader must interpolate data to determine what happened, and extrapolate data to predict what will happen.

- When turning the information into the model:
  - ✓ The information developed from the data allows the leader to iteratively develop, over time, a model or strategic picture.
  - ✓ The strategic picture allows the leader to understand and explain what is happening to the organization in the current environment.
- The search for inflection points, where the data and the current model diverge, is never ending.
- The leader must constantly be on the lookout for data that suggest the current model is no longer able to solve the most intractable problems of the day, indicating a change in paradigms is needed, and/or the technologies or processes implementing the paradigm are disruptively changing, indicating a change in technologies or processes is required.

For visual representation of this summary, see Figure 12.

WHAT AM I GOING TO DO DIFFERENTLY ON MONDAY?

- I will set aside fenced thinking time about my data, my information, and my model.
- I will assess whether I am getting the right data with the right frequency without drowning.
- I will evaluate whether the data I am getting is filtered or inaccurate.
- I will pick a failure or success and do a deep dive to determine the information in that failure or success.
- I will ask myself weekly, "What just didn't happen here?"
- I will consider alternative data interpretations to avoid the seductive easy or quick answer.
- I will search for signs of inflection points in the paradigm or the processes/technologies.

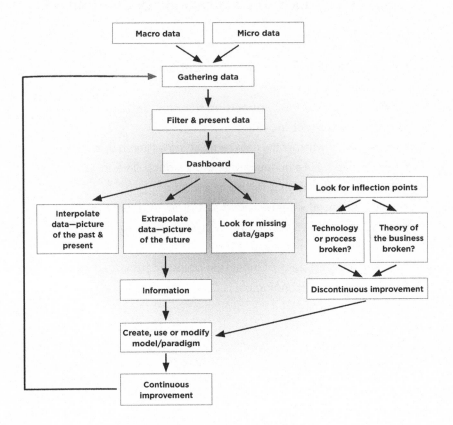

Figure 12

VISIONING

Visioning

5

The leader uses the strategic picture to create a vision of the future and develops the attendant dynamic strategies.

This vision and the strategies drive systemic transformation and continuous improvement.

The leader is the Chief Visionary.

How does the model/strategic picture connect to the vision?
The model/strategic picture describes the present.

The vision describes a desirable and achievable future.

While you can have a vision without a model or strategic picture, it's difficult to create strategies if you don't know where you're starting from.

Why dynamic strategies?
For any given vision, there are multiple strategies that can be created to achieve that vision. There are many choices to get to where you want to go.

Not only are there many choices, but strategies can and must change as the situation evolves. Therefore, the strategies must be dynamic.

Which is it, systemic change or continuous improvement?
That depends.

If the organization is fundamentally healthy, and there is no disruptive or systemic change on the horizon, then you are looking for continuous improvement.

If the organization is broken or there is disruptive or paradigmatic change on the horizon, then you need systemic transformation.

And it's usually both!

Who creates the vision?
There is often considerable confusion as to whether the vision springs wholly formed from the brow of the leader or is created by a small group of zealots operating near independently.

The answer is both, and neither.

Who creates the vision is not as important as having a vision that is consistent with the model/ strategic picture.

> The only visioning absolute is that if the leader is not intimately involved with the creation of the vision, then the vision and the attendant strategies are doomed.

The only visioning absolute is that if the leader is not intimately involved with the creation of the vision, then the vision and the attendant strategies are doomed.

Ideally, the leader will be involved in the creation of the vision, given that it is the leader's mental model that drives the vision. The leader must absolutely have final approval of the vision.

Why do you need a vision?
The answer to this question seems intuitively obvious. Yet the

number of organizations that have either an outdated or halluci-nogenic vision is legion.

If the leader does not have a vision, then many on the leader's team will set a vision, or no one will set a vision.

If there are multiple visions within an organization, the odds are high that they will conflict or leave gaps. If there is no vision, then you have random organizational motion. In either case, strategic chaos ensues.

How do you create a vision?

As the Chief Sensor, the leader developed a mental model, a strategic picture of the present, based on data and information.

This model describes the past and present, and is a result of deep and thoughtful observation over a consequential period.

But the model does not describe the future. That is the purpose of the vision.

The leader should share the strategic picture with her organi-zation and stimulate intense contemplation about what the model says about both the present and the future.

The vision describes where she wants to be at some point in the future.

While not always the case, visions usually have a temporal component, describing some time frame for achievement.

A vision should be aspirational. If the vision is easy to get to or you're already on a path to the vision, then you'll probably have a tough time selling the vision or motivating people to sacrifice to achieve it.

The vision must be relevant—it must address the issues raised by the model and the realities of the current environment.

While the vision is aspirational, it should not be halluci-nogenic. An unrealistic vision will only frustrate your team.

The vision can be incremental. If you have a complex and long change in your future, then having multiple incremental visions over an extended period is just fine. But you can only have one vision at a time.

Finally, the vision must be easy to understand. Preferably, the vision is a short as possible. I subscribe to the principle of KISS—keep it simple and short.

Vision drives change, and therefore the vision must be (over) communicated

Vision will drive change.

There are many excellent books on how to change, but my favorite is John Kotter's *Leading Change*.

Kotter breaks down the change process into eight steps. The most important step for the leader is to communicate the vision once she has signed off on that vision.

> **Change is hard, brutally hard, and if people don't understand where you want them to go, they will be disinclined to do the hard and extra work necessary to achieve the vision.**

Change is hard, brutally hard, and if people don't understand where you want them to go, they will be disinclined to do the hard and extra work necessary to achieve the vision.

The leader is not only the chief visionary but also the chief communicator of the vision. Communicating the vision should become all-encompassing for a consequential period. Kotter, in his analysis of change failures, identifies under-communicating the vision by a factor of 100 or 1,000 as one of the keys to failure.

Vision drives the strategic plan

One of the most common errors made in strategic planning is to commence the strategic planning process in the absence of a clearly articulated vision.

The data and the observation of the past and present drive the model. The model, the strategic picture, drives the vision. The vision drives the strategic plan.

As any math student will tell you, there are an infinite number of paths between two points. Strategies are nothing more than vectors that take you from the present to the future, from the model to the vision. And you can choose from many paths.

What does a simple process for creating a strategic plan look like?
An incredible amount has been written about strategic plans and strategic planning. Many people have tried to make it an art form, sometimes even a religious experience. But it's inherently sim-ple—strategic planning is about getting from the present to the future.

Start with your mission, which is what you do, who you do it for, and how you do it.

You must understand your environment, so add a description of the environment—those things that are beyond your control. Often, SWOT analysis is used to analyze strengths, weaknesses, opportunities, and threats (SWOT).

The vision is where you want to be at some point in the future. It is achievable and aspirational, but not hallucinogenic. It should have a time horizon.

Strategies are the macroscopic actionable steps you will take to get from the present to the future, given the environment in which you operate.

You can rarely achieve what you can't measure. Strategies are measured by metrics, and vision is gauged by outcomes.

Strategies do not happen in a vacuum. Priorities are the order in which strategies are accomplished, while guiding principles are the non-negotiable patterns of behavior—culture! We will look at cultures in detail in chapter 6.

So there you have it—in figure 13, one graphic that simply describes the strategic planning process.

Realistically, it's a lot more complicated, but the principles are easy to understand, if not always easy to execute.

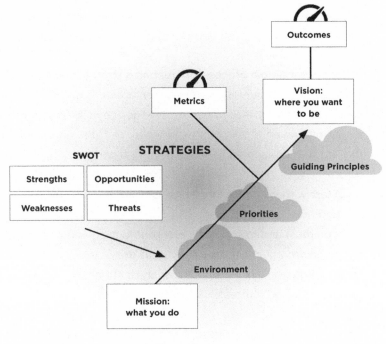

Figure 13

What is the relationship between strategy and work plans?

Both as a consultant at Booz|Allen|Hamilton and as the leader of the Pacific Fleet Process Improvement Team, I had the opportunity to see many visions and strategic plans.

Frequently, we encountered strategic plans that were extremely detailed and of significant length. In fact, these "strategic plans" looked suspiciously like work plans.

The fundamental distinction between a strategic plan and a work plan often causes organizational confusion.

By definition, a strategic plan should be written at a high level, and it is usually quite concise—something that everyone in the organization from top to bottom should be able to understand and speak to.

By definition, a work plan is detailed and extremely specific to subsets of the organization. A work plan should be able to answer who does what, by when, at what cost, and assign specific metrics that indicate accomplishment.

You know you're in trouble when...

Based on decades of looking at strategic plans and working with many teams to create them, I've compiled my top 10 moments when "you know your visioning and strategic planning are in trouble."

1. The vision is more than one relatively short sentence.

2. The vision is generic and could be applied to any organization.

3. The leader cannot coherently articulate the strategic picture or the vision in under 30 seconds. The leader cannot discuss in detail, for at least 15 minutes without notes, how she came up with the vision and how she hopes to achieve it.

4. The receptionist doesn't know or cannot articulate the vision.

5. The strategic plan is more than two pages long and/or is gathering dust on a shelf.

6. The folks in the cubicles don't know their part in the strategic plan.

7. Metrics and budget do not correlate directly to the strategic plan and the vision.

8. The strategic plan has not been updated or modified in at least a year.

9. There is no work plan.

10. The work plan is not dynamic, not specific, and hasn't been updated in at least one month.

CHAPTER SUMMARY

- The leader creates a vision of the future and its attendant strategies.
- The vision describes a point in the future that is aspirational and realistic.
- The vision must be relevant and easy to understand.
- While you can only have one vision at a time, that vision may, and probably should, evolve.
- The vision drives systemic transformation or continuous improvement, and sometimes both at the same time.
- Strategies describe how you are going to get from the present to the future.
- There are an infinite number of strategies, and they take into account the environment, guiding principles, and priorities.
- Strategies are dynamic and not static.
- Strategies are measured by metrics, and vision is measured by outcomes.
- The strategic plan is not a work plan, and a work plan is not a strategic plan.
- The work plan is a detailed document, applicable to specific subsets of the organization, that answers who does what, by when, at what cost, and assigns specific metrics that indicate accomplishment.

For visual representation of this summary, see Figure 14.

WHAT AM I GOING TO DO DIFFERENTLY THIS *QUARTER*?

The astute reader will notice that I changed the time frame from "what am I going to do differently on Monday" to "what am I going to do differently this quarter."

That is because creating the vision is by definition less tactical and therefore less short-term, and therefore the time frame for actions is longer.

- If my organization does not have a vision, I will cause the organization to create one (soon).
- If my organization does not have a strategic plan, we will use the vision to create one (soon).
- If we have a strategic vision, I will check to see whether it is driving action throughout the organization.
- I will demonstrate my personal involvement and passion for the vision and its implementation.
- I will assess and reassess our strategies to determine whether they are still relevant, and change our strategies as necessary.
- I will examine our metrics and outcomes to see whether we are making progress and take action if we are not moving forward.
- I will review the work plan at least monthly.
- I will review the strategic plan at least quarterly.

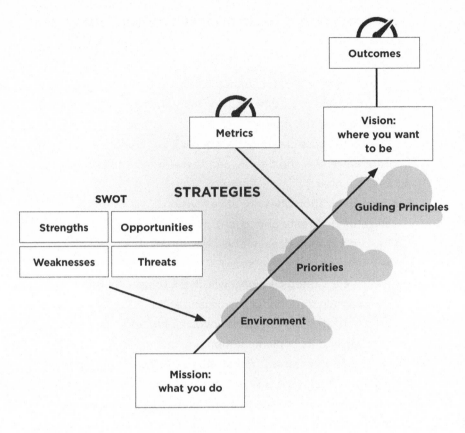

Figure 14

ACCULTURATION

Acculturation

The leader sets and owns the culture of the organization.

The leader is the Chief Cultural Officer.

Who, me?

If there is one idea that is extraordinarily difficult for most leaders to understand, and more importantly to implement, it is that the leader owns the culture of the organization.

Culture is easy to ignore—until it's too late. It's rarely written down. It's very difficult to measure; there are few if any "culture meters." It's incredibly difficult to change.

All of which means that there can only be one person in charge of culture—the boss! Which is precisely why it's one of the non-delegables.

Okay, so what exactly is culture?

While there are many formal definitions, I define culture as the norms of behavior that govern what people in the organization will do and how they do it, even when no one is looking.

Another frequently used definition of culture is that it is the sum total of the values of the organization.

> **I define culture as the norms of behavior that govern what people in the organization will do and how they do it, even when no one is looking.**

It's relatively easy to conform to cultural norms in public. Many can talk the talk.

Ideally, the behavioral norms espoused by the organization, the culture, are the same in public and behind closed doors. Regretfully, that's not the case in many organizations, where people pay lip service in public and do whatever they please in private. And that's why I added the suffix phrase *even when no one is looking.*

What exactly is *our* culture?

One of the first questions asked by a prospective leader during the onboarding process should be "What is our organizational culture?" Regretfully, the answers are usually all over the map—everyone *thinks* they know the organizational culture.

That should drive the prospective leader to ask the second, more difficult, question about the organizational culture: "And how do you *know* what the organizational culture is?"

If the leader has grown up within the organization, he likely has a reasonable idea of the culture. As a cautionary note, he may understand the culture as he has seen it and may become confident that he knows the culture throughout the organization. But in many cases, culture is not uniform, particularly across the geographic or age spectrum.

> **Everyone *thinks* they know the organizational culture.**

If the leader is coming from outside the organization, it is critical that he rapidly gain a deep understanding of the culture. A cultural assessment, often by an impartial outside organization, should be part of the onboarding process.

Is the culture the same throughout the organization?
Absent a strong unifying culture that comes from the top, there can be as many different cultures as there are organizational units. And absent a unifying culture, the subcultures can clash, sometimes dramatically, to the detriment of the organization. This is another reason why culture must start at the top, driven by the leader.

Is culture outward facing or inward facing?
The answer is almost always "both".

How you treat your team and how you treat your customers should be absolutely consistent with your culture.

If there is a discontinuity between the internal and external culture, that is a fundamental problem that needs to be corrected. Immediately.

Assessing the culture as Chief Sensor
In his role as the Chief Sensor, the leader develops the model/strategic picture. Painting an accurate picture of the culture and behavioral norms is vital, since it directly impacts the implementation of the vision.

For example, if the culture of the organization is focused so strongly on sales that ethics take a backseat, the first thing the leader must do is change the culture—so that ethical behavior becomes the norm, not the exception.

> **It will be difficult to make progress toward a grand vision until the culture is aligned with the vision.**

It will be difficult to make progress toward a grand vision until the culture is aligned with the vision.

Where does it say what the culture is?
I am a strong proponent of articulating the culture in writing. This is not easy. Your written statement will not cover every

eventuality, but being able to point to a piece of paper that articulates how you want people to behave is a powerful tool to influence behavior.

A written statement of culture is also a powerful tool to help you, the leader, behave consistently with your own guidance. As CEO, I published a one-page document, *The CEO's Philosophy*, and hung a framed copy in my office, in plain view, right above the portrait of my family, directly in my line of sight. I encouraged, even demanded, that my team hold me accountable to that philosophy. Because we are all fallible, it is easy to deviate, inadvertently, from your cultural direction. Having your team help you stay on track is a powerful tool and reinforces your commitment.

I have included a verbatim copy of my CEO's philosophy as appendix 2. Even though some portions are tailored to an organization working for doctors, those portions can be scaled to any organization.

It's about boundaries

One way of thinking about culture is as a set of boundaries. If you're inside the cultural boundaries, you are behaving appropriately. When you cross the lines of a cultural boundary, your behavior is inappropriate.

Immutable boundaries

Basic ethical norms—fixed boundaries—do not change, whether you're the janitor or the CEO. These boundaries are usually easily defined and very clear. For example, "We will not lie, cheat, or steal." I refer to these as immutable boundaries.

> **Basic ethical norms— fixed boundaries— do not change, whether you're the janitor or the CEO.**

One of my frequent questions when deciding an issue was to ask out loud, *"Is this option illegal, unethical, or immoral?"* While I usually already knew the answer, it served as a verbal touchpoint to make sure all those involved in the decision, particularly myself, had explicitly answered those three immutable boundary questions.

Philosophical boundaries

Some boundaries are clearly written, but open to interpretation. In many cases, they are deliberately open to interpretation to allow for initiative and flexibility. For example, "We will do what's right for the customer." These are philosophical boundaries.

In the days of sail, the Royal Navy would dispatch their frigates on independent operations for months, sometimes years. The Royal Navy's Articles of War were the immutable boundaries—they were clear, absolute, and inviolable. But, in the absence of long-range communication, the Admiralty would give the captain detailed guidance, usually referred to as Sailing Directions, covering most, but not all, situations. If the Sailing Directions were well written, they would begin with philosophical guidance—giving the overriding objective. It was up to the ship's captain, far from home, far from someone telling him what to do, to interpret the philosophical guidance in the best interests of king and queen.

Think of Commander Jack Aubrey of *HMS Surprise* in the movie *Master and Commander.* The first line in his orders was to sink or destroy the French commerce raider, *Acheron.* In the fine print of his orders, it told him not to go past a certain point in the South Atlantic. Because his philosophical boundary—to destroy *Acheron*—trumped all else, the captain deliberately violated the fine print and pursued *Acheron* into the Pacific.

I encourage you to adopt a similar attitude. Give your team the immutable boundaries—those ethical and legal norms whose violation you will not tolerate under any circumstances—like the Royal Navy's Articles of War. Then give them the philosophical guidance that governs their behavior when discretion is both authorized and needed—if you will, the Sailing Directions from the Admiralty.

It should be obvious that the leader's philosophical guidance must be nuanced and thoughtful. The guidance that Dilbert's pathologically awful leader gives is designed only to protect him in case things go wrong. It's the epitome of leaders giving bad guidance.

Think very carefully about the philosophical guidance you give to your team. Let them have as much flexibility as possible without allowing them to do something really stupid.

Calibrated boundaries

Many boundaries are not open to interpretation but can be changed based on either circumstance or the individual. For example, "At this level in the organization, you may approve purchases up to $5,000." I refer to these as calibrated boundaries.

For example, as CEO I had a dollar limit beyond which I could not independently sign checks. I likewise established a dollar limit for my team, based on their experience and the needs of their job. The boundaries were calibrated to either the individual or his level of responsibility.

How is a calibrated boundary different from a rule or a regulation? If the calibrated boundary does not shape culture, it is simply another rule in a big, fat book of rules. But you can send a good (or bad) message using calibrated boundaries. For example, I wanted to encourage independent thought and behavior in my small team at the Medical Society. I gave everyone a credit card and allowed any team member to charge, without prior approval or second-guessing, up to $500 for any reason they considered consistent with our strategies and vision.

The boundaries and the culture at work

Another sea story is in order. My first ship, *USS Nautilus*, was the oldest submarine in the fleet and therefore a real engineering challenge. *Nautilus* was the first nuclear-powered submarine, so there were some design quirks that were fixed on subsequent classes of submarines. We were proud of the fact that we kept *Nautilus* going along all the way to her 25th anniversary, as Admiral Rickover promised Congress when he built *Nautilus* in the 1950s.

Many, many years ago, during a port visit, I was assigned as the engineering duty officer on arrival in port. Since we were tied up to the pier and connected to shore power, the propulsion plant was shut down. The ship's duty officer and I waved goodbye to the entire wardroom, captain and all, as they left the ship to storm the beaches!

Late that evening, the shore power breaker opened and despite everyone's best efforts, refused to stay shut, causing us to lose our external source of electrical power.

We were now on the horns of a dilemma. Because of *Nautilus'* design, we had unpleasant choices. We could keep the reactor shut down, but because of the immutable laws of physics, force the ship to later do something that would land us on the front page of the local paper and on every local TV station. Not a good idea!

Or we could start up the reactor.

Our conundrum was that starting up the reactor required the captain's permission. After all, we were junior officers, and starting up the reactor was the captain's exclusive prerogative. And in the days before cell phones, contacting the captain was not an option.

Our absolute boundary was to keep the ship and the reactor safe, in that order.

The philosophical boundary that Commander (later Admiral) Dick Riddell taught us was to always do the right thing—for the ship, the Navy, and the nation.

The calibrated boundary was that we did not have the authority to start up the reactor—both the captain and Admiral Rickover's rules were very, very clear: only the captain could grant permission. And Admiral Rickover was notoriously cranky about people violating his rules!

After a short discussion about boundaries, we started up the reactor because the absolute boundary and the philosophical boundary trumped the calibrated boundary.

We consciously exceeded our authority because doing so would keep the reactor safe and avoid embarrassing the ship, the Navy, and the nation.

Captain Riddell's culture was "do the right thing, and I will back you up." The next morning, after everyone had filed back onboard after an exhausting night on the beach, we dutifully reported our actions, half expecting to get fired for a gross violation of the standing orders.

> **The *Nautilus* culture that Captain Riddell created resulted in behavior that, while he was not there, allowed his team to make the right choices.**

Nope. The captain thanked us, and we went about our business. And we never heard boo from Admiral Rickover.

The *Nautilus* culture that Captain Riddell created resulted in behavior that, while he was not there, allowed his team to make the right choices.

How are boundaries defined?

The obvious way is through words. Writing boundaries is easy. The first iteration of defining culture is usually through written rules as boundaries. But defining culture and boundaries through the written word is only the first step.

For example, I articulated my philosophy—my ethical norms and guidance—in writing. This document is included as appendix 2 for your use as you see fit. It was difficult to live up to every day, but it was a goal that steered me in the right direction.

Behavior, particularly by senior members of the organization, and specifically the leader, either reinforces the written word or renders the written word irrelevant.

For example, if integrity is a stated cultural norm for the organization, but the CEO's travel claims are inflated, that gets out very quickly—and destroys any attempt at making integrity part of the culture.

When I was the Engineer Officer of the *USS Pogy*, I would

routinely stand watches in the nuclear power plant with my officers-in-training. We were required to do a pre- and post-watch tour of the propulsion spaces. Every so often I would locate debris in the bilges or find a lightbulb that was out or blinking. Sometimes my young trainees would walk past these minor anomalies, either because they missed them or because to their untrained eye it wasn't a big deal. It didn't take long for them to get my message when I wordlessly got down on my hands and knees and picked the detritus out of the bilges and handed it to them.

In a similar vein, I once saw a two-star admiral ask for a flashlight during an inspection of a submarine, get down on his hands and knees in his dress white uniform, and shine a light on the filth behind a commode in the crew's head (bathroom). Everybody got the message!

> **Boundaries and culture may be defined by words, but they are reinforced by the actions of the leader.**

Boundaries and culture may be defined by words, but they are reinforced by the actions of the leader.

Lights, cameras, action—roll culture!

The leader is on stage 24 hours a day, seven days a week, and 365 days a year. Everyone looks at you, all the time, in everything you do, to see what cultural norms the leader embodies—and even more importantly, which cultural norms the leader violates. Even when you're shopping at Costco, you're on stage!

> **The leader is on stage 24 hours a day, seven days a week, and 365 days a year. Everyone looks at you, all the time, in everything you do, to see what cultural norms the leader embodies.**

As the leader, you simply cannot evade the limelight. Ever.

Boundaries and your team

While it is the leader's job to set

the boundaries, there are four responsibilities for members of your team.

First, never cross immutable boundaries.

Second, cross philosophical boundaries only when there's a damn good reason.

Third, work with the leader to expand your calibrated boundaries. Continuously demonstrate to the leader that your boundaries deserve to be expanded, based on your performance, and you will likely see them expanded.

Finally, help the boss stay on the right side of the cultural boundaries.

As a very junior CEO, I nearly made an embarrassing and unethical choice. In public, in haste and in error, I directed the most junior member of my team to do something that was clearly out of bounds. She pointed out to me, in public, that my idea was dumb and unethical (she was much more tactful than that). It took real courage for her to take on the boss in public. Thankfully, she did. But it was also something I had specifically given every member of my team permission to do—actually, I told them I expected it of them. See appendix 2, "Honesty." And I thanked her, in public, for keeping me on the straight and narrow.

Every leader will make mistakes—you have to depend on the culture you created to keep those errors in check.

Every leader will make mistakes—you have to depend on the culture you created to keep those errors in check.

The three-sided square

One of my mentors, retired Navy Captain Jeff Fischbeck, espouses the three-sided square when he thinks about boundaries. If you bound behavior on three sides of a square, but leave the fourth side open, typically people will move in the direction where there are no boundaries. This is a clever way of getting the behavior you want while still having limits.

How do you teach someone to safely moor a multi-thousand-ton submarine at the pier? There are so many variables—wind, current, location, room, water depth, weather, timing, available pier support, tug configuration, and more. To learn how to safely moor, a young officer, under the watchful eye of the captain, is allowed to make all the propulsion, rudder, line handling, and other orders necessary to reach the goal of a safe landing. He can do all of this without intervention from the captain—if it's within established or perceived limits of acceptable action (i.e., within the boundaries of the three-sided square), and in the right overall direction (the square's open side). If all goes well, the captain says little or nothing. If things don't go well, then a teachable moment happens.

Good judgment comes from experience, and experience comes from bad judgment.

Good judgment comes from experience, and experience comes from bad judgment. The three-sided square keeps bad judgment safely contained.

But won't these boundaries kill initiative?
On the one hand, you want to encourage initiative and aggressiveness. On the other hand, you want people to work within the boundaries, not outside them. This is a fine line for both the leader and the team.

If people understand your vision, then the vision should provide them with the big picture of what they need to do.

Providing additional philosophical guidance will help them do the right thing when you're not around. That's why well-written philosophical boundaries are so important.

And that's why listening closely to your team is so important – they will, albeit subtly, tell you when your boundaries need to be changed.

Communicating with your boss

The good news is that today you can talk to your boss from almost anywhere and at almost any time. The ability to communicate should minimize crossing boundaries while trying to achieve the vision.

In the Navy, I was frequently put into the position of making critical decisions in the middle of the night, when all my seniors were asleep. My first commanding officer, the aforementioned Dick Riddell, gave me a superlative piece of advice when he certified me as a watch officer. He told me to call him, wake him, when in doubt.

> *"When in doubt, call. When in doubt about being in doubt, call,"* **is a great way for the leader to encourage initiative and aggressiveness while still maintaining some control and not allowing subordinates to cross boundaries.**

When I was in doubt about being in doubt ("do I *really* want to wake him about this..."), it was absolutely time to call the captain. To him, the only unforgivable sin was ignoring that little voice in the back of your head that was telling you "maybe you should talk to the boss about this."

You cannot cover every eventuality in written or verbal guidance.

But, the dictum I learned on *USS Nautilus*, "When in doubt, call. When in doubt about being in doubt, call," is a great way for the leader to encourage initiative and aggressiveness while still maintaining some control and not allowing subordinates to cross boundaries.

CHAPTER SUMMARY

- The leader sets and owns the culture of the organization.
- Culture is defined as the norms of behavior that govern what people in the organization will do and how they do it, even when no one is looking.
- Culture is defined by a series of boundaries.
- There are three types of cultural boundaries:
    - ✓ Immutable boundaries—deeply rooted ethical norms or organizational values.
    - ✓ Philosophical boundaries—clearly written top-level guidance that is open to interpretation.
    - ✓ Calibrated boundaries—direction not open to interpretation which can be changed based on either circumstances or the individual.
- The leader must have an accurate sense of the culture in the organization and change it as appropriate.
- Changing culture is hard, long, and painful.
- Vision cannot be achieved unless and until the culture is aligned with the vision.
- Articulate the culture you desire in writing.
- Cement the culture you desire with your behavior.
- The leader can never evade the cultural limelight.
- Encourage your team to call you if in doubt, and more importantly, to call you if in doubt about being in doubt.

For visual representation of this summary, see Figure 15.

WHAT AM I GOING TO DO DIFFERENTLY ON MONDAY?

- I will ask to see the most recent cultural assessment of my organization. If no recent assessment exists, I will commission one.
- I will review my immutable, philosophical, and calibrated boundaries.
- If I have not articulated my boundaries, I will do so in the next month.
- I will reflect, in writing, on how my behavior is reinforcing or degrading the culture I desire for my organization.
- I will ask a trusted partner, an influential customer, and my top three direct reports to send me a one-page document that evaluates the culture of our organization.

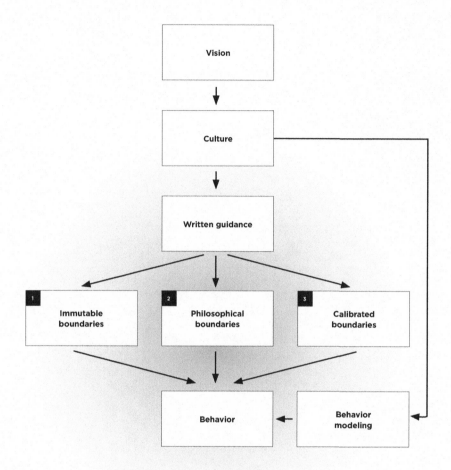

Figure 15

ENABLING

Enabling

7

The leader enables their team by providing them with all the tools necessary to implement the vision.

The leader is the Chief Enabler.

Paging Dilbert...

You've created the vision based on the model. Strategies and vision statements are printed and on everyone's desk. You've started to move the cultural needle. You're done, right?

> **The moment where progress comes to a screeching halt is when people are asked to implement vision and strategies without the necessary tools.**

All too often across the spectrum of businesses and organizations, the moment where progress comes to a screeching halt is when people are asked to implement vision and strategies without the necessary tools.

There is a reason that the cartoon strip *Dilbert* is a favorite of the cubicle clan. *Dilbert* articulates the recurring frustration of team members who are asked to do more and more with either the same or less. Teams are excruciatingly frustrated because they understand the vision (most of the time), they see the strategies (usually but not always), yet they are empty-handed when it comes to getting the work done.

Why is this a leader responsibility?

The odds are slim that you the leader are going to be turning wrenches, recalculating spreadsheets, or drafting documents that do not directly support the vision of the organization. Unless the organization is exceedingly small, you've told people where you want them to go, and then you got out of the way.

> **It is your responsibility to make sure that people have what they need, where they need it, when they need it, to achieve your vision.**

But getting out of the way is the wrong answer.

It is your responsibility to make sure that people have what they need, where they need it, when they need it, to achieve your vision.

Notice I said *your* vision. Until and unless your team owns the vision, it is just that—your vision. And they won't own it if they don't have the tools they need to implement it.

It is critical to establishing ownership of the vision throughout the organization that you follow up your grand words and soaring vision with concrete actions—give people what they need to get to where you want them to go. Enable success!

What do they need?

I believe there are seven broad categories of enabling and tools.

First, and probably most important, you and your team need a culture that supports the implementation of the vision. It's been said many times, and I will repeat it here for emphasis:

culture trumps strategy 100 percent of the time. If your culture does not support the implementation of your vision, your vision won't happen. I discussed acculturation in much more detail in the previous chapter because I maintain that the leader is the Chief Culture Officer.

Second, you need people. But you also need the right people. You need the right number of people. In some cases, but not all, that means increasing headcount. In others, it means redirecting your human resources.

Third, your team needs hardware, software, and tools. For example, trying to build a website on a dial-up modem is a recipe for resignation and failure.

Fourth, they need the financial resources. It's trite but true: no money, no mission, and certainly no vision.

Fifth, they need priority. Reflecting on what *Dilbert* has told us, you cannot have 10 priority-ones. Something, singular, must be first in line. Multitasking is a wonderful idea, but research and experience have shown that you can usually accomplish one difficult task at a time. If the implementation of your vision is not first in line, the results are predictable.

Sixth, and probably most nuanced, your team needs process and predictability. That doesn't mean creativity and innovation are outlawed, but it does mean that you have stable and repeatable processes.

Finally, your people need knowledge and skills. They need to have access to the information necessary to make the changes, and the personal skills necessary to translate the information into action.

Does the culture support the vision?

If the culture of your organization does not support a change in the vision, then your number-one priority is to create a culture that is supportive.

That's why, although culture is one of the categories of tools,

I treat culture separately from the other tools and name it as one of the seven non-delegable roles of the leader, give it a separate chapter, and discuss it before the remaining tools.

Do I have the right people to implement the vision?

What got you here won't necessarily get you there. Likewise, the people that got you here won't necessarily be the people that get you there.

You as the leader need to carefully assess whether you have the right people in the right places with the right skills and in the right numbers necessary to implement your vision.

And this may require a significant change in personnel. Much has been written about a brilliant visionary who is stymied by an inner circle that does not understand or support where the leader wants to go. It is amazing how often the wrong people are tolerated under the wishful thinking that maybe they'll come around. While it sometimes happens, it is rare to find people who can make dramatic shifts in organizational philosophy.

Surround yourself with people who support the vision. And I don't mean tepid tolerance; those that surround you, organizationally and physically, must be in full-throated public and private support of your vision and strategies. Be ready to rapidly change your inner circle if they are unwilling or unable to support the vision.

Make sure you have the right number and the right type of people at the worker level to implement the vision. That's easily said, difficult to implement, and usually takes much longer than desired. Once your inner circle is to your liking, each member of that inner circle needs to replicate the process with their inner circle, and so on ad infinitum. Complicating the process is that it may be much more difficult to change personnel the farther you are away from the C-suite. However, selective and highly public promotion of those who embody your vision sets a powerful example and can speed up the process.

Making sure you have the right people throughout the organization is a process of positive mentoring and Darwinian selection. Thousands of pages have been devoted to the "how" of selecting the right people—the techniques. I would encourage you to read *First, Break All the Rules* by Marcus Buckingham and a weekly column in *The New York Times*, "Corner Office." Both of them give excellent insights into technique.

> **While technique is important, the most important part of picking your team is finding partners who passionately support implementing your vision.**

While technique is important, to me the most important part of picking your team is finding partners who passionately support implementing your vision.

Do they have the right tools?

I invariably got quizzical looks when I posited that the leader needs to make sure the right tools are in the hands of the right people. I would have to explain that I didn't mean the leader was down at Home Depot buying things at the Tool Corral (except, of course, for projects at home!).

The coach of a football team would never ask the team to compete in this era with leather helmets. Yet, there are innumerable examples, humorous and sometimes tragic, of people being asked to do complicated and challenging things with outdated, ineffective, or dangerous equipment.

It's the leader's job to make sure, to delegate and to verify, that her people have the tools they need to execute the vision.

> **It's the leader's job to make sure, to delegate and to verify, that her people have the tools they need to execute the vision.**

Talking about tools is particularly challenging for the leader because it sounds suspiciously like micromanagement. Why should the leader get involved in selecting an Internet Service Provider (ISP) for a web design firm? The answer is not necessarily that they should be involved in the selection of and contracting for the ISP. Rather, the leader must make sure that someone is, in fact, doing this, and to listen when her team complains about the slow Internet.

I was expansive, even profligate, about making sure that my team had the hardware and the software they needed to get the job done right.

Data is the lifeblood for any membership organization. Shortly after coming onboard in 2001, I asked to see SDCMS' IT systems, including the hardware and software we used to keep track of our precious members. I didn't know whether to laugh or cry when my well-intentioned team showed me an IBM 36 sitting in the back of the office. To put this in perspective, the IBM 36 was cutting-edge hardware in the 1970s. When I asked to see how we obtained usable data, I found a non-relational, non-programmable, flat file spreadsheet. Needless to say, we quickly and very publicly replaced hardware and software so that we could compete effectively.

Do they have money?

Implementing a new vision is not free. To get the tools, to hire the people, and to rearrange the priorities, resources will almost surely have to be adjusted.

> **Many try, and most usually fail, to implement a new vision on the cheap.**

Most leaders know that they will have to shift resources to achieve a vision. Regretfully, many understand the principle, but then don't actually shift resources.

Many try, and most usually fail, to implement a new vision on the cheap.

Does implementing the vision have the priority?

The clearest signal from the leader to the team that implementing the vision is important is an overt rearrangement of priorities. Allocating the three previous enablers—people, tools, and money—is a very clear signal of the priority the leader places on implementing the vision.

There is an old maxim, "Watch their feet, not their lips." Talk is cheap, but actions telegraph the

> **The clearest signal from the leader to the team that implementing the vision is important is an overt rearrangement of priorities.**

truth. This is where the leader can make or break the implementation of a new vision. Your people will very quickly determine whether you are all talk and no action. In addition to communicating the vision, your priorities have to be clearly and publicly articulated and reflected in people, tools, and money.

Two simple yet powerful tools can help. First, look hard at your schedule. Are you spending your precious time on work directly related to implementing the new vision? I used color coding on my calendar for items directly related to strategic planning and implementation. That helped me stay focused and prioritized very publicly my commitment to the vision. Second, I asked every member of my team to publicly list their top three priorities. Obviously, if those top three priorities did not align with vision and strategy, that became easily correctable. More importantly, during my walk-about time, I would discuss *their* priorities and *their* progress on *our* priorities, and how that connected to the strategy and vision of the organization.

> **The leader has to be fearless in canceling or eliminating activities that drain precious resources and do not relate to achieving the vision.**

If you're going to embark on a consuming strategic initiative, ask yourself, "What are we no longer going to do?" Institutional inertia is powerful. Organizations and people are loath to get rid of programs and processes that they've been doing for a long time. But the litmus test "Will this help us accomplish our vision?" should be applied to all processes and commitments. The leader has to be fearless in canceling or eliminating activities that drain precious resources and do not relate to achieving the vision.

When I came on as CEO, I had a graphic in my office of a sacred cow in the background and a big red X in the foreground. People got the message!

Later in my time as CEO, I brought the graphic closer to my line of sight, because some of the sacred cows that needed slaying were ones I had created!

Are the processes repeatable and predictable?

One of my favorite sayings is "Improvise, Adapt, and Overcome," popularized by the gruff Marine gunnery sergeant played by Clint Eastwood in the movie *Heartbreak Ridge*.

Improvising, adapting, and overcoming are terrific traits, but it's difficult to run an organization *in the long run* as improv theater. The larger the organization, the lower the tolerance for unpredictability.

It is the responsibility of the leader to ensure that the organization's processes are repeatable and predictable. The leader must walk a fine line to ensure that while the processes are stable, those same processes are not ossified and not a hindrance to progress.

> It is the responsibility of the leader to ensure that the organization's processes are repeatable and predictable.

Systems failures are a typical indicator that processes are not well regulated, so it behooves the leader to ask "why" when things don't go right.

While there are always exceptions, the great majority of systems failures are not because you have bad people, but because you have bad processes. Riffing on James Carville in the 1992 presidential election, *"It's the processes, stupid."*

And it is up to the leader to insist that processes be in place and that these processes are repeatable and predictable.

And when processes fail, the diagnosis and corrective action for failures is usually a teachable moment.

Do people have the knowledge?

There are two ways of looking at knowledge that will enable your team to implement your vision.

There is personal knowledge. While knowledge and skill are not necessarily the same, to enable your team, the team members need to have the knowledge and skill for the tasks at hand. This dovetails with having the right people, the second enabler.

But there is a more nuanced perspective on having knowledge. For your team to be truly creative in support of the vision, they must have access to all the information they need. The patron saint of bad leadership, the pointy-headed boss in *Dilbert*, is infamous for

> **Your team will not be effective if there are secrets or hidden information that will result in their inefficient approach to a solution.**

sending his team on a mission that cannot be accomplished because he holds back vital information. Your team will not be effective if there are secrets or hidden information that will result in their inefficient approach to a solution.

How do you know?

The role of the leader as Chief Enabler is twofold:

First, either give the people the tools or direct that the people receive the tools. That is the easier of the two.

Second, verify that people have the tools they need. This is the real work of leadership. This is where you must constantly check to see whether the direction you provided to enable the vision is happening.

Checking that you have enabled your team is a great topic for Management by Walking Around (MBWA). Making a habit of talking to everyone in your organization and asking them whether they have what they need is a wonderful educational experience for the leader, and a real loyalty builder. When people see you talking to your team and asking them, probing and questioning them, whether they have what they need to implement the vision, that sends a clear message.

Two notes of caution are applicable to the MBWA concept. First, never shoot the messenger. While you may not like the message, it takes exactly one temper tantrum for word to get out that telling you the truth is not a good idea. Second, investigate before acting. Not everything you are told on the shop floor is necessarily accurate, so look (carefully evaluate the information you've been presented) before you leap (act).

When you find out that people don't have what they need, that becomes a closely watched teachable moment.

If you find out that for whatever reason your people don't have what they need (including other people), everyone will watch carefully to see whether the situation changes.

If they report a deficiency and things get quickly rectified, that communicates that implementing the vision is a priority.

Alternatively, if they tell you they need more tools and nothing appears, that communicates that implementing the vision, despite all the talk, is really not a priority.

CHAPTER SUMMARY

- The leader enables their team by providing all the tools necessary to implement the vision.
- The team needs culture, people, tools, money, priority, processes, and knowledge.
- The leader is directly responsible for providing a culture that supports the vision. Chapter 6 is entirely devoted to the leader as the Chief Culture Officer.
- Since culture trumps strategy every time, if the culture will not support change, stop almost everything until the culture is fixed or is well along in the process of being fixed.
- While the leader is not directly responsible for procuring people, tools, money, priority, processes, and knowledge, the leader is responsible for ensuring these enablers are adequate and available for the team.
- The leader should inspect frequently and talk to their team often to make sure that the team does have the right culture, people, tools, money, priority, processes, and knowledge.
- The leader must be extremely aggressive in correcting a lack of enablers. Failure to provide what the team needs sends a clear signal that implementing the vision is not important to the leader, and it will quickly doom a change effort.

For visual representation of this summary, see Figure 16.

WHAT AM I GOING TO DO DIFFERENTLY ON MONDAY?

- I'm going to meet weekly with one or more of my teams and probe whether they have what they need to achieve the vision.
- I will ask my COO or deputy to review the adequacy of the six enablers: people, tools, money, priority, processes, and knowledge.
- I will pick up a copy of *Dogbert's Top-Secret Management Handbook* and thumb through it to see whether I have some of the horrible traits of the pointy-headed boss, particularly with enabling my people.
- At least monthly, we will look to see what processes or tasks we will no longer do.

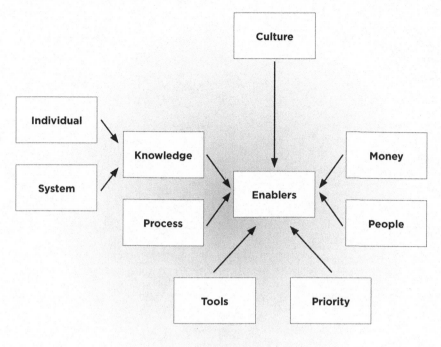

Figure 16

DECIDING

Deciding

The leader makes the right decisions in the right way at the right time.

The leader is the Chief Decider.

No kidding...

For eons, leadership has been about making decisions—from a Neanderthal chief picking which cave to winter in, to Hannibal masterminding the annihilation of eight Roman legions at Cannae with a ragtag pickup group half their size, to Henry Ford inventing the mass production of the automobile, to Steve Jobs creating the iPhone by sheer will.

The reader can justifiably express that leadership is obviously not a delegable role and certainly does not deserve a chapter. After all, leaders make decisions! Next chapter, please.

Well, not so fast.

Making the right decision

As the leader, your menu of possible decisions is nearly infinite. Being an effective leader is about picking those decisions that you are going to make that most significantly impact your organization's vision and strategies.

While nothing keeps the leader from choosing the carpet pattern in the headquarters building, I believe that there are much more important strategic decisions to be made—for example, whether to own a headquarters building or even to have a headquarters.

> As the leader, your menu of possible decisions is nearly infinite. Being an effective leader is about picking those decisions that you are going to make that most significantly impact your organization's vision and strategies.

I believe the leader should delegate almost all decisions that are not related to vision or strategy to his team. That requires the leader to have a clearly articulated vision and strategy that he can use as a filter for deciding whether to take on a certain decision.

Steve Jobs was fanatical about details that everyone around him thought were irrelevant. He was always able to link decisions about (apparently) minor details to his vision of the iPhone as supremely user-friendly.

Commander (later four-star admiral) Archie Clemins, the captain of my third ship, *USS Pogy* (SSN 647), spent a ridiculous amount of time on the appearance of the ship's Weapon Shipping Hatch (WSH) and Operations Compartment Upper Level (OPSUL) passageway. When in port, the *only* way onto the ship for visitors was to come down the WSH and walk through the OPSUL passageway. Woe to the duty officer who allowed this area to degrade to anything less than absolute gleaming perfection. Why, his officers asked, do we have to be meticulous to the point of absurdity about this one area? Because, he patiently explained, the first impression every visitor has of our ship is the WSH and OPSUL. In his folksy downstate-Illinois way, he described the WSH/OPSUL as his front porch—and if your front porch is a mess, the odds are your garage and the rest of your house are a mess, too! Continuing with the metaphor, having a messy house (a slovenly submarine) would have been extremely detrimental to the reputation of the ship. His decision to focus some of his precious attention on what seemed a triviality was really about his vision to project his ship in the best light. And by the way, the rest of the ship was pristine too, because we came to understand his philosophy and vision!

Decide what you're going to decide

The leader gets to decide what he decides. It's not a tautology—it's about picking those high-impact decisions where you will make the final decision.

As the Chief Sensor, you developed a fundamental understanding of the organization and its environment and created the mental model of what's important. Anything that affects the big cogs in your mental model is something you should choose to make decisions on.

For example, if you're the CEO of Ford, you want to be the final arbiter of the company's direction considering the clear and present danger to your business model from Tesla Motors.

If you're the Secretary of Defense, you want to make sure you are the decider on which of many high-cost weapon systems you're going to purchase given limited budgets and multiple present and future threats.

If you are not going to decide, then delegate who will

Again, it's another one of those obvious things. But if you choose not to make a type of decision, then explicitly delegate who will make that particular type of decision and determine what the important parameters of that decision are.

Different decisions are made using different processes

It's not enough to know *what* you're going to decide. It's just as important knowing *how* you're going to decide.

> It's not enough to know *what* you're going to decide. It's just as important knowing *how* you're going to decide.

Many books have been written about decision processes, and it is not my intent to duplicate them here.

But I found that the clarity provided by David Snowden and Mary Boone in their seminal *Harvard Business Review* article "A Leader's Framework for Decision-Making" was very useful as I decided how to decide.

Snowden and Boone lay out four possible contexts for deciding: the simple, the complicated, the complex, and the chaotic.

The simple context—known knowns

In the simple context, we are in the domain of best practices. There is usually a single right answer.

But just because the decision is simple does not make the decision easy. It takes at least a decade to train a physician to surgically repair a case of appendicitis, even when the diagnosis is obvious.

In the simple context, the leader should avoid oversimplifying or being complacent by misclassifying a decision. Given that there is usually a single right answer, the leader should avoid micromanaging. And best practices, the usual correct answer, can change, so the last best practice may not be the current best practice.

Simple decisions should, in general, be delegated.

The complicated context—known unknowns

The complicated context is the domain of the experts, since there are usually multiple correct answers. Paraphrasing then-Secretary of Defense Donald Rumsfeld, we are dealing with known unknowns. We know what we don't know.

For example, when an organization has outgrown its current footprint, there are multiple options to obtain more space—you can buy it, you can lease it, you can build it, or you can choose not to expand at all. There is a lot of expertise that can advise the growth decision, but in the end, the leader must decide on only one path.

The leader will eventually have to choose from one of several possible answers presented by the experts. The leader should be aware of tunnel vision by the experts, should listen to the experts but still encourage novel thinking—maybe the experts aren't the only ones with good ideas!

> **The leader has to make the trade-off between finding the perfect right answer and forward motion—avoiding the paralysis of analysis.**

The leader has to make the trade-off between finding the perfect right answer and forward motion—avoiding the paralysis of analysis.

Finally, the leader needs to sense if decision-making is taking too long or the answer is elusive. In either of those cases, then perhaps the process of decision-making is incorrect, and he should be looking at a different decision-making process—the complex decision.

The complex context—unknown unknowns

The complex context for decision-making is the domain of emergence and unknowns. Again paraphrasing Rumsfeld, we have unknown unknowns. There are no right answers—yet.

San Diego's public utility decided to plug into renewable solar and wind energy generators in the desert 100 miles from downtown. How to route the high-tension wires over very challenging mountainous terrain was a complex decision. Many stakeholders, many factors, many regulations, and many conflicting needs had to be incorporated. There was no blueprint to consult; they had to invent the blueprint.

Paraphrasing Harry Truman, only the really tough calls land on the boss's desk. Making a complex decision is a tough call because of the ambiguity and multiple variables associated with the decision. This is where the leader really demonstrates his decision-making mettle.

The leader needs to experiment—to allow the path to reveal itself. Probing, questioning, being patient, forcing people outside their comfort zone—these are all part of making a complex decision.

Beware of falling back into directive management because of the frustration of not finding an answer quickly; rather, demand from your team an experimental mode of management. You are trying to make a decision without knowing all the questions, never mind the answers.

But also appreciate that your initial decision on a complex matter may be wrong because no one knows the right answer. Changes of direction are normal as more of the problem reveals itself and better options become apparent.

The chaotic context—the unknowables
This is the domain of chaos and turbulence. It requires a rapid and accurate response. There is little if any analysis, only instinctive response. This is the classic command-and-control mode.

For example, on 9/11, then-Mayor Rudolph Giuliani gave orders – there were no long-winded committee meetings. In the first 24 hours, his role was to direct the restoration of order.

The leader is only trying to restore order. The leader must stop the literal or figurative bleeding—to move away from chaos.

This is an area where the leader must be directive. Delegation is not the right answer in the chaotic decision-making context.

Your team expects you to be in charge. They need you

to be in charge. They will look directly to you for the answers during the chaos.

President George W. Bush had two opportunities to be in personal charge. On 9/11 he went to New York as soon as possible and asserted to the nation that he was in charge with a megaphone, standing on a pile of rubble. The nation came together under his leadership. After Hurricane Katrina, he flew over New Orleans in Air Force One, then returned to Washington, and was then roundly criticized for not being in charge.

The leader should also beware of staying in command-and-control mode too long and becoming a legend in his own mind.

Who decides - you or them?

In addition to differentiating decision making by the nature of the problem, you can differentiate decisions by who makes them. There are two broad categories – the solo decision, where you alone decide. Alternatively, there is the collective decision, where the group essentially makes the decision.

The collective decision—listen to everyone, but...

One of my favorite leaders at the Medical Society, Dr. Stu Cohen, had a great way of making a collective decision. He would convene his brain trust and ask everyone for their opinion, starting with the most junior member of his cabinet. He would insist on a recommendation or a comment from each person present. After everyone had spoken, he would announce what he felt was the consensus, his tentative decision, and his reasoning. Then he asked who could not live with that decision, and why. After having heard everyone, he announced his final decision (which was usually, at that point, a consensus decision). Everyone felt like they had a voice, and while not everyone agreed, they understood and supported him. He made the final decision, but he clearly identified consensus and followed the group.

The solo decision—listen to the brief, but...

Sometimes you will make a decision without a collective process. Usually, such a decision will be preceded by a brief from your subordinates, either orally or in writing.

I insisted that both the written and the oral brief answer five basic questions:

- ✓ What do you want me to do?
- ✓ Why do you want me to do that?
- ✓ What's in it for me (really, what's in it for the organization)?
- ✓ How long will it take?
- ✓ How much money will it cost?

Retired Vice Admiral Charlie Martoglio taught me the sixth question, proving that you can teach an old dog new tricks!

- ✓ What else do I need to know to make a good decision?

That last question forces the hands of subordinates who may not be forthcoming with pertinent information. Once subordinates know you're going to ask, they tend to put everything on the table up front.

Once I received the brief to help me decide, I asked three things, out loud, to myself:

- ✓ What's the right (moral) thing to do here?
- ✓ How will this decision impact our constituents - the people I worked for?
- ✓ Is the decision consistent with our vision and strategies?

Oh for Pete's sake, make the doggone decision!

All of us have experienced bosses who are incapable of deciding. For these non-leaders, there will always be more facts to obtain, more meetings to be held, more people to consult, ad nauseam!

In the Navy, we created the caricature of the drowning commander who, when thrown two life jackets, couldn't decide which one to put on, and perished.

At some point, you have to decide!

Umm, why did we do that?

After making the decision, an effective leader shares his rationale and his decision-making process with, at a minimum, his senior staff. If it has wide-ranging impact, the leader should discuss his decision-making process widely.

Particularly for difficult decisions with negative consequences for members of a team, it is critical that the leader spend time ensuring everyone gets an explanation. The leader is not asking for concurrence (because the decision has already been made), nor is the leader going to allow re-litigating the decision. Rather, he is giving an explanation and asking for understanding. Knowing that your decision was not capricious is important to your team.

As well, explaining your process helps senior members of your team understand your decision-making process, and becomes a teachable moment for you as Chief Mentor.

Who gets to make what decision?

I recommend that as Chief Enabler, you make processes repeatable and document them. As Chief Decider, when it comes to decision-making, I recommend that you identify in writing those decisions that only the leader will make.

> If the leader will not make the decision, then the leader should delegate who will make those kinds of decisions.

If the leader will not make the decision, then the leader should delegate who will make those kinds of decisions.

And be extremely careful about making ad hoc or snap decisions. Regretfully, you can easily set a precedent that will be hard to break. Two great questions to ask yourself when you are tempted to make a first-of-its-kind decision are:

- ✓ Why is one of my subordinates not making this decision?
- ✓ Do we (really) need to make this decision right now?

Yeah, it's hard!

General Norman Schwarzkopf, the architect of Desert Storm 1, famously said, *"Knowing the right thing to do is easy, but doing the right thing is hard."*

Accept that making difficult decisions is hard. Sounds obvious, but acknowledging the difficulty is part of dealing with it.

If making hard decisions starts to become easy, that's a signal that you may be becoming callous or jaded, and you need to rethink your role as leader.

As a former boss used to say, *"Nothing hard is ever easy."*

OK, so how did we do on this deciding thing?

Except if a decision ends in catastrophe, very rarely is the decision-making process critiqued and evaluated.

> Get in the habit of looking in the rear-view mirror at your decision making and learning from it!

It is your prerogative, and I believe your responsibility, to insist on evaluating all major decisions for both process and efficacy.

Get in the habit of looking in the rear-view mirror at your decision making and learning from it!

And be hard on yourself, not your people.

It's a privilege

In all my years of being in charge, I always felt leadership was an earned privilege, but a privilege nonetheless. In making the big decisions in the right way at the right time, I was able to make a tangible difference in people's lives and, in my small way, affect the direction of the nation and my community.

When I retired from the Medical Society, I wrote in my valedictory that one of the things I would miss was the privilege, as Chief Decider, to fix, prevent, or annul stupid stuff.

My father was an officer with the mountain troops during World War II. Because of the horrific officer losses of these elite warriors, where the dictum was that officers lead from the front, he started as a platoon leader and ended the war as a battalion commander. He rarely spoke of his experiences, but when he passed away, I inherited his war diary. I co-dedicated this book to him because his love and care for his troops and the passion of his decision-making under the most extreme circumstances were palpable, and they remain an inspiration to me even today.

Make the right decisions in the right way in the right time.

And treasure the privilege of making a difference through those decisions.

CHAPTER SUMMARY

- The leader makes the right decisions in the right way at the right time.
- The leader gets to pick which decisions he makes and delegate the rest.
- Different decisions are made using different processes.
- Listen to everyone, but make the decision.
- Communicate both the decision and how you made it to everyone involved.
- Deciding is hard, sometimes devilishly difficult. Yet it's a privilege to make a difference.
- Some great questions to ask:
  - ✓ What do you want me to do?
  - ✓ Why do you want me to do that?
  - ✓ What's in it for me (really, what's in it for the organization)?
  - ✓ How long will it take?
  - ✓ How much money will it cost?
  - ✓ What else do I need to know to make a good decision?
  - ✓ What's the right (moral) thing to do here?
  - ✓ How will this decision impact our constituents - the people I work for?
  - ✓ Is the decision consistent with our vision and strategies?
  - ✓ Why is one of my subordinates not making this decision?
  - ✓ Do we (really) need to make this decision right now?

For visual representation of this summary, see Figure 17.

WHAT AM I GOING TO DO DIFFERENTLY ON MONDAY?

• I will review or commission a review of the last three major decisions my organization made, looking for efficacy and process.

• I will identify in writing all the decisions that are exclusively my purview.

• I will identify two pending decisions—one complex and one complicated—and evaluate the process of decision-making.

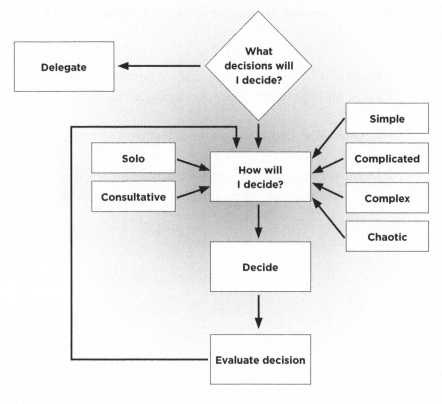

Figure 17

EMBRACING

Embracing Responsibility

The leader embraces responsibility for everything in their organization.

Which is it—accepting or embracing?
As I was crafting the paradigm, I used the phrase "accepts and embraces responsibility". But as time went on, I realized there was a significant difference between the two verbs. Accepting and embracing are not the same thing. Accepting is a passive perspective on responsibility, driven by either statute or custom. Embracing is an active perspective that drives proactive behavior. The leader must do both, but I focus on the proactive embracing. In fact, the whole point of this book is to help leaders to be proactive in their roles.

Paging Atlas, now paging Atlas!

The trappings of being the leader are seductive—the prime parking spot, the big office, not having to fly peasant class, the largest paycheck in the organization, and so on... But there are reasons and a cost for those privileges.

> **The weight of your world is indeed on your shoulders. The leader must learn to embrace this weight.**

Unfortunately, like Atlas, the weight of your world is indeed on your shoulders. The leader must learn to embrace this weight.

If you accept but cannot embrace the weight of responsibility, you are in the wrong line of work.

If you resent the weight of responsibility, then you need to look deep within yourself, and either change your mindset or find something else to do.

It's only lonely if you choose to make it so

A frequently heard saying is that it's lonely at the top.

I would argue that is not completely accurate. You are lonely at the top only if you choose to be. Having an intimate circle of advisors, even friends, on whose opinion you rely is critical. Having someone outside the organization who can mentor you is likewise vital.

As CEO, I had an incredibly productive and positive 11-year partnership with my COO, James Beaubeaux. During our final one-on-one interview before hiring him, we agreed on three simple partnership rules: I would not try to be the COO, he would not try to be the CEO, and there would be no-none-zero-zip secrets between us. We consulted each other about every, and I do mean every, decision. While the responsibility for the Medical Society was all mine, he supported me in every way possible, and his friendship and support made the responsibility less of a burden. I encourage you to find your James Beaubeaux.

Peer mentoring and peer relationships are likewise a vital support mechanism to help you carry the load. Find a group

You can never ever delegate responsibility.

of close advisors and meet with them regularly, whether formally or informally, while insisting on two things—honesty and confidentiality. If they cannot tell the emperor that he has no clothes on, then it's not the relationship you want. And if they cannot keep the conversations private, then it's likewise not a productive relationship.

While the final decision and responsibility rest with you, there is nothing wrong with having others reinforce you as you hold up the weight.

It may not be lonely, but it is absolute

You can share and delegate a lot of things, including adversity and joy, but the responsibility is yours alone. And it cannot be parsed or divided or allocated. You can never ever delegate responsibility.

Responsibility does not equal micromanagement

A common misconception is that being responsible for everything means you must manage everything and delegate nothing. Not so.

First, you do not have the bandwidth to manage everything, particularly as the organization grows beyond the nominal span of control of about 7 to 15 people.

Second, if you're managing everything, your people are managing nothing.

Third, if you're managing everything, all the critical functions and roles that we've talked about so far are not getting fulfilled.

In fact, the whole purpose of writing this book is to make sure you're spending the most precious resource of the organization, your time and your focus, on those things that other people should not or cannot do.

Embracing responsibility means focusing on those things that have critical impact

Since you cannot manage everything, you need to be extremely selective about that for which you take personal time and attention.

Picking those things that will receive your personal attention is a very delicate balancing act between risk and reward.

If you are personally managing things that do not have the potential to get the organization into trouble, or things that will not help you achieve your vision, then you're probably looking in the wrong spot.

> The whole purpose of writing this book is to make sure you're spending the most precious resource of the organization, your time and your focus, on those things that other people should not or cannot do.

Think of your personal attention as a flashlight in a large, very dark room known to contain predators. If you are looking at the floor for cockroaches, you will find them, but the cockroaches are not going to kill you. You need to be looking with that flashlight for the predators. That means for the predators. That means you must think about and plan for where you expect the predators to be. And then point the flashlight there, not at the cockroaches.

And make sure that you and your leadership circle are pointing your flashlights in different directions.

When I was second-in-command of *USS Gurnard* (SSN 662), my commanding officer and I had an ironclad rule. If he and I, the two most senior and experienced officers on the ship, were both looking at the same thing, something else wasn't getting the attention it needed. Submarining is an inherently dangerous business, but the extreme competence of the officers and crew mitigate that risk. In early 2000, we took *Gurnard* from San Diego to the North Pole and then circumnavigated the North American continent by returning home through the Panama Canal. Early in the trip, as we were transiting the Bering Straits in winter (we were going north, the icebergs were going south, both in extremely shallow water), the captain and I were enjoying a brief respite in the wardroom. Suddenly, a casualty was announced over the loudspeakers. I will never forget the next 30 seconds, because without a word, he and I sprinted out of the wardroom in exactly opposite directions, each of us going to a control station to handle the casualty, but on opposite ends of the ship. While training and experience allowed us to deal with the issue safely, having the two most experienced officers onboard pointing their figurative flashlights in different directions was crucial.

The degree of delegation

The size of the organization determines, in a macroscopic sense, how much can or should be delegated. However, the leader has a great deal of control over the degree of delegation within a certain sized organization.

What you delegate, or conversely that which you do not delegate, telegraphs a great deal about you, your style, and your focus.

Responsibility and authority

In almost every situation, with responsibility comes authority. The leadership challenge is knowing when to use your authority, and to what degree. Regretfully, the world is filled with leaders who abuse or overuse their authority, and with leaders who treat their authority as radioactive. Balancing between over- and under-use of authority is a constant challenge that becomes easier with experience.

With responsibility comes authority. The leadership challenge is knowing when to use your authority, and to what degree.

One of my favorite examples of an appropriate use of authority came during an external audit of our repair facility on *USS McKee*. We were given a list of things that needed to be fixed, including some high-priority items. Captain Tom Etter, who had just assumed command, directed that the urgent items be corrected by Monday morning (it was late on Friday afternoon). The relevant officer expressed concern and frustration, not particularly kindly, about this get-it-done-now direction. Captain Etter raised his eyes over the top of his reading glasses, looked straight at the relevant officer, and very evenly and very quietly said, "Monday will be fine," and continued to read the report. Everybody in the room got the message, and it wasn't just about Monday morning.

For two years I chaired a meeting for my statewide association of independent medical society CEOs. My first board meeting did not start well, when one of my fellow CEOs threw a temper tantrum early in the meeting. I knew that if I tolerated this behavior once, it would go on for the next two years. I also knew that, while I had no direct authority over the partic-ipants, I had the authority as chair to manage the meeting. I quickly gaveled a recess, and then had a very calm and deliberate conver-sation with the CEO. I told him that as chair, I would never recognize him again (effectively silencing him in perpetuity) if he ever did that

> The fundamental conundrum of leadership in this incredibly complex and interrelated world is that you must learn to give up a great deal of control. Yet you are still responsible for everything.

again. He smiled (he was just testing how far he could go with the new kid!), acknowledged, and we thereafter developed a very productive working relationship. I had the responsibility and authority, and I used that authority in a deliberate and appropriate way—for the good of the group.

Wait a minute—I'm responsible for everything, and you want me to delegate almost everything?
The fundamental conundrum of leadership in this incredibly com-plex and interrelated world is that you must learn to give up a great deal of control. Yet you are still responsible for everything.

At this point you are probably thinking, "Mr. Gehring, you must be joking!" and you are ready to toss this book in the trash.

I don't blame you. But hold on for just a bit longer.

The trick is to recognize the conundrum, accept the inherent contradiction, and read this book carefully.

Intelligently give up that which is not central and then make sure that what you gave up stays under control.

Intelligently give up that which is not central and then make sure that what you gave up stays under control.

Nobody ever said leadership was easy! Rewarding, yes. Easy or simple, no.

So, WHAT do I delegate?

Thinking deeply and proactively about the Venn diagram of what you do and do not delegate is one of the hardest and most necessary things the leader must do.

You could either first decide what to delegate to your team, and therefore everything else belongs to you; or you could decide what is non-delegable and belongs only to you, and conclude that everything else belongs to your team.

You can approach this in one of two ways: you could either first decide what to delegate to your team, and therefore everything else belongs to you, as in figure 18; or you could decide what is non-delegable and belongs only to you, and conclude that everything else belongs to your team, as in figure 19.

The two approaches can be graphically represented as follows. In figure 18, I first highlight the large circle (that which I will delegate), which then by exclusion defines the smaller circle (that which I don't delegate).

In the second case, figure 19 below, I first highlight the small circle (that which I don't delegate), which then by exclusion defines the large circle (that which I delegate).

My approach, and the genesis of this book, was to decide first what belonged only to me (the non-delegables), and therefore conclude that everything that did not belong to me was delegable.

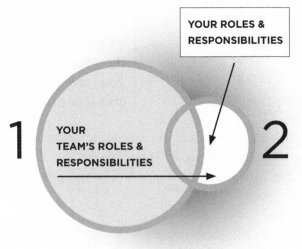

Figure 18

And how do I delegate?

How to successfully control *your* part of the Venn diagram, *your* roles and *your* responsibilities, is the focus of this book.

That leaves the obvious question of how you manage that which you do delegate. There have been many books written about effective delegation, but to me it's relatively simple.

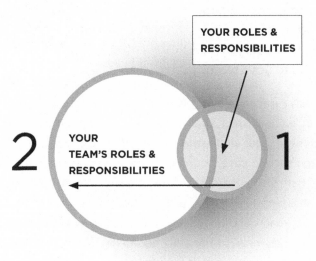

Figure 19

Set a tripwire or a boundary

The key to successful delegation is to delegate authority and set tripwires. A tripwire is a boundary where action is taken when the boundary is breached.

The leader must tailor the authority delegated as a function of the strength, talent, maturity, experience, and dependability of the person to whom she is delegating. As well, the consequences of failure have to be factored into the boundaries or tripwires of delegation.

> **The key to successful delegation is to delegate authority and set tripwires.**

Setting a boundary, just like we talked about in culture, means allowing your subordinate freedom within a defined space. However, the subordinate is not allowed to exceed a boundary without action and/or notifying you. Clearly mark boundaries, allow your subordinates freedom within those boundaries, and designate the required action if they approach or exceed the boundary.

A nautical example illustrates this point. While the ocean is vast, the possibility of collision between ships at sea is always present, and as my good friend Ron Mathieu always reminded us, *"A collision at sea can ruin your whole day."*[3]

Millennia of experience have taught mariners that, to avoid a collision, they should never let another ship approach within a certain radius. The watch officer is given great latitude to operate the ship without contacting the captain. However, he is required to call the commanding officer whenever another ship could or has breached that safety radius.

The captain has delegated authority but has set boundaries where she is to be called, or tripwires where action is mandated.

In the post-mortem to nearly every at-sea collision, the common thread is a failure to take action within a certain range, and failure to involve the leader when hazard approaches. While the watch officer

---

3. The debate about whether this saying is attributable to Thucydides occupied many a wardroom dinner, but the sad truth is that attribution to the Greek historian is a hoax.

is usually sanctioned after a collision, it is the commanding officer who is held ultimately responsible and accountable.

In this example authority has been delegated, boundaries and a tripwire have been set, but responsibility has been retained.

Agree on the delegation Venn diagram!

Once you've decided on your delegate/no-delegate strategy, formalize it.

> Once you've decided on your delegate/no-delegate strategy, formalize it.

It can be as simple as my handshake agreement with my COO—after all, we were a very small organization. It can be as complex as detailed responsibility charts for a huge organization.

But have the conversation with your subordinates, agree on the Venn diagram, and codify it.

Don't blame the subordinates—ever!

There isn't much quite as pathetic as a leader who blames something in her organization on a subordinate. Yes, the subordinate screwed up. But it was you or your people who picked the subordinate, allowed him to stay on, authorized the systems and processes that did not catch the problem, or failed to build the systems and processes that would catch the mistake.

On my last sea tour on *USS McKee*, a very large floating industrial repair facility, we were involved in very delicate work on submarine propulsion plants. During one particularly intricate repair, a watchstander allowed a critical system to fail. Through good design, the backup system kicked in and prevented catastrophic failure. But allowing any critical system to fail was a major problem. Everyone was ready to blame the watchstander. After all, he had fallen asleep on watch, one of the cardinal sins in any military organization. We were ready to call the hanging judge, metaphorically of course!

When we asked "why, why, why, why, and why," we put the

figurative hanging on hold. Yes, he had fallen asleep on watch. But the errors committed by his chain of command created a situation that made his failure all but inevitable. After having returned from vacation at 8 AM, and without any prior notice, he was informed that he was going to stand watch from midnight to 6 AM on a station on which his qualification had lapsed. And then his leadership team kept him working from 8 AM to midnight. And they didn't make sure he was familiar with the equipment. Yes, Superman would not have fallen asleep on watch. But it was the leadership team that was responsible for his failure, not him. And it was the leadership team we held accountable

Black Swans

Rarely, very rarely, there are "black swan"[4] events that you just cannot plan for, no matter how smart or proactive you are. But be very leery of thoughtlessly assigning a problem to the black swan category. And if it truly was a black swan event, ask yourself how you would preclude it the

> **Failure was my responsibility, and success belonged to the team.**

next time. And constantly be thinking about black swans!

Who are you going to blame?

I had a simple protocol when dealing with success and failure. Failure was my responsibility, and success belonged to the team.

Why? Why? Why? Why? Why? Why?

Since you are responsible, you have the privilege of asking "why?" until you get to ground truth.

In disciplines that involve life or death, there are formal processes for finding and fixing the root causes of disaster. In

---

4. A black swan event is an event or occurrence that deviates beyond what is normally expected in a situation and is extremely difficult to predict; the term was popularized by Nassim Nicholas Taleb, a finance professor, writer, and former Wall Street trader. Black swan events are typically random and are unexpected.

medicine, there is a process called the Morbidity and Mortality Conference. On submarines, we had formal critiques, with a mandated process for getting to the truth. And all of us are familiar with the National Transportation Safety Board (NTSB) determining what happened, and why, in aircraft accidents or mishaps.

Hopefully you will not be facing life-and-death decisions in your role as leader. However, you have the authority to convene an investigation when things don't go right. I cannot overemphasize the importance of determining the root cause of everything that didn't work out the way you planned.

And while diagnosing failure is not fun, you should not limit your investigations to just when things go wrong. When things go right, identifying success enablers will help you replicate them across the organization.

In chapter 3, I talked about the pre-mortem. This is a brilliant technique conceived to prevent the long faces, finger-pointing, and shaming/blaming when things don't go according to plan. The essence of the technique is to proactively think about potential

> A leader with real foresight will convene a pre-mortem to prevent a post-mortem.

problems and how to avoid those problems, and then take specific steps to prevent likely points of failure.

A leader with real foresight will convene a pre-mortem to prevent a post-mortem.

You are the face of the organization

Part of being responsible is that to the outside world, you are the face of the organization. When something great, or something awful, happens, your team and the outside world expect you to be front and center.

The fun part, of course, is to be handing out awards, receiving recognition, and being introduced as the leader of a successful organization. Enjoy!

Sooner or later, hopefully later or never, something not good will happen, whether it is a public relations crisis, a major gaffe that winds up in the media, or just having to report unpleasant news. You need to be prepared to stand tall in front of the cameras, and your peers, and your team.

It is the height of cowardice to send out a subordinate to report the bad news.

Got a plan?
Another part of being responsible is planning and thinking about cataclysmic events.

Particularly for awful things like disasters, it is critical to have a plan that you've rehearsed. It is not a question of whether something bad will happen while you are a leader, but just a question of when and where.

The proactive leader will ask what the most likely bad things might be, then prioritize them on a two-by-two matrix: likely/not likely, catastrophic/not catastrophic.

After prioritizing the list, the forward-thinking leader will do three things for the high-priority potential problems, those that are both likely and catastrophic:

First, convene an action group to proactively avoid the high-priority potential problems—an ounce of prevention is worth a pound of cure.

Second, develop a well thought-out and rehearsed plan on what do if the problem materializes.

Finally, the proactive leader will convene a task force to think about the unthinkable—the aforementioned "black swan". Their charter is to think and act to prevent things that are so far outside the norm as to be initially considered implausible.

For 10 years, a committee of the Medical Society had been working and thinking about infectious diseases, both natural and man-made. They had prepared organizationally for a microbial onslaught without knowing the precise pathogen we would actually see. The membership of the committee was spread throughout all the major San Diego hospitals. In October 2001, six weeks after 9/11, the United States was in the middle of an anthrax scare. SDCMS was able to publish a 10-page bioterrorism primer in an amazingly short time. This primer allowed San Diego hospitals (and we shared the primer statewide and nationwide) to be appropriately and rapidly prepared for whatever came next. We did not know the exact time and shape of the actual event, but our preparation helped us rapidly and effectively respond.

Authority and responsibility, and making a difference.
With responsibility comes authority. With authority comes the ability to make change for the better (or, regretfully, sometimes for the worse).

I encourage you to use the authority that comes with your responsibility to make your part of the world a better place.

The real joy of leadership is knowing that you've made a positive difference. There is nothing more rewarding.

CHAPTER SUMMARY

- The leader accepts and embraces responsibility for everything that happens in her organization.
- It's lonely at the top only if you choose to make it so. Partners, friends, peers, and mentors all make the burden easier to manage.
- You cannot delegate responsibility.
- What you choose to delegate (other than responsibility) is the central question of leadership.
- Clearly define the Venn diagram of what you do and do not delegate.
- Delegate authority, but set boundaries and tripwires.
- Don't blame subordinates—look in the mirror!
- Investigate the root causes of success and failure.
- You are the face of the organization, in good times and in bad.
- Plan for the avoidance and handling of disaster.

For visual representation of this summary, see Figure 20.

WHAT AM I GOING TO DO DIFFERENTLY ON MONDAY?

- I am going to pick a recent success or failure and direct a deep dive into its root causes.
- I am going to find one specific task, role, or responsibility that I am going to delegate.
- I am going to cause an audit of delegated critical functions and ensure that there are appropriate tripwires and boundaries.
- Once a month, I am going to call up a mentor, friend, or partner and schedule an informal lunch or breakfast to chat about leadership.
- I am going to ask to see my organization's disaster plan.
- I am going to commission a highly capable "black swan" team to assess potential disasters, specifically including "oh-that-would-never-happen-here" events.
- Once or twice monthly, I am going to meet with one subordinate and have an honest and deep discussion about what is delegated, what the boundaries are, and what the tripwires are for his team.

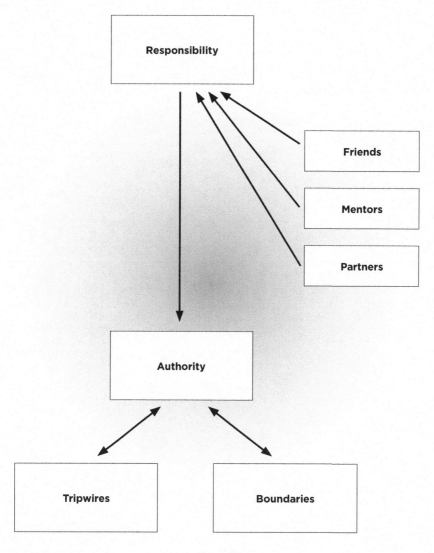

Figure 20

MENTORING

Mentoring

10

The leader selects, trains, and mentors the next generation of leaders.

The leader is the Chief Mentor.

Figure 21

And the circle is unbroken. There is a reason that the last of the seven non-delegable roles is right next to the first on the master graphic. Even as you start your journey, know that it will end. You as the leader are responsible for ensuring that the next generation is ready, and in fact better than the current generation.

My wife, Cathy, shot the photo of figure 21 as my then four year old son and I were walking in the mountains near San Diego.

If you look closely at his hands, you will see that one is holding mine and the other is indicating we are engaged in an animated and intense Socratic conversation.

That young tyke, whom I mentored since he was two years old, is now an adult of whom I am very proud, and to whom this book is co-dedicated.

By teaching we learn!

You are the Chief Talent Scout

But what is talent? One of the books I recommend is *First, Break All The Rules*, by Marcus Buckingham. He asserts that we normally look for three things when we bring new people onboard: knowledge, skill, and talent. Knowledge is what you know. Skills are what you know how to do. Talent is what you have the potential to do in the future.

You can neither teach nor learn talent.

Creating the next generation of leadership means finding those talented individuals, either inside or outside the organization, who will do great things for either the organization or the world at large.

It means holding their hands (figuratively) when they are junior, engaging them in animated Socratic discussions to teach them, and then letting go of them when they are ready.

Just like in the picture of my son and me.

You are the Chief Sower of Seeds

Talent is inherent but sometimes hidden. Many talented people do not realize just how good they are or could be. This is true for many reasons, most of them not very good—bad previous bosses, poor opportunities, societal factors—the list is long and not pleasant.

But if you see a bright glimmer of talent, as the sower of seeds your role is to help people realize they are talented.

Whether inside your organization or in the community at large, incubating talent is part of your role as a leader.

The first time I got underway on *USS McKee*, I noticed that all the officers and enlisted bridge watchstanders were long-serving and very competent—and 100 percent male. But my officer and enlisted contingent was one-third female. I inquired not very tactfully as to why there were no women standing senior watches.

Needless to say, the answer was not acceptable. So we embarked on a two-year program to identify the talented but heretofore unqualified female officers and enlisted who, for whatever reason, had not been offered the opportunity. Not all of them reached the pinnacle, standing underway watch officer, but every one of them was afforded the opportunity. One of my proudest moments occurred several years later when we got underway with an all-female bridge watch section!

We had turned "No, I can't do that because of ... [insert lousy excuse here]" to "Wow, this is cool—I can do this!"

Just like me 15 years earlier on that howling winter night in the cockpit of *Nautilus*, they were exhilarated and terrified. And they had been well taught. The circle had indeed closed.

You are the Chief Mentor

Mentoring is different than sowing seeds.

Once you have found someone and she starts to blossom, part of your responsibility is to help her grow into something bigger, something more capable, and help her fulfill her potential.

Mentoring means taking an active interest in her career and involves spending consequential one-on-one time with the mentee.

In addition to being incredibly rewarding, mentoring is another non-delegable role of the leader.

Obviously, there is a finite bandwidth, and you cannot mentor everyone. But you should mentor someone!

You are the Chief Career Counselor

While mentoring and career counseling are related, they are not the same thing.

Career counseling means that you find specific tailored opportunities, whether educational or job-related, for your talented next generation that help them grow to their potential.

You are the Chief Role Model

If your people want to be like you, that's a great thing.

You can learn many things from great leaders.

If people watch your behavior and vow never to be anything like you, that's a bad thing.

You can learn great things from awful leaders.

Succession planning

You must have a short-term succession plan.

It does not and should not mean that you get to handpick your successor. But it does mean that you need to be ready for transition—whether it is today, next week, next year, or next decade.

The French leader Charles de Gaulle pointed out that the graveyards are full of indispensable men. Despite what everyone tells you, the organization will survive without you.

In the short term, you must be able to answer the question "What happens if I, the leader, get hit by the proverbial bus, or my airliner re-validates the laws of gravity? Who will carry on for a 6- to 12-month time frame?" Every organization must have a short-term succession plan so that someone, usually but not always your second-in-command, can hold down the fort long enough for a long-term successor to be identified and brought up to speed.

Likewise, you must have a long-term succession plan. When do you plan on moving on? Based on that, what is the plan for having at least one or two fully qualified internal candidates to take your place?

Look outside your organization

Nowhere is it written that you are limited to mentoring and teaching only within your organization.

The world is full of talented people crying out for mentoring. I firmly believe—in fact, the reason I wrote this book—that you must always be leaving the world a better place than you found it, and one of the best ways to do that is to help talented individuals grow to their full potential.

Many years after I departed the submarine service, I was invited to attend a submarine's change-of-command ceremony. A senior commander whom I had mentored as a very young officer was completing his command tour. I was brought to tears when he singled me out from the podium for the mentoring and teaching that I had done almost 15 years earlier.

> **Invest the time today to teach the next generation. It will be one of the most rewarding things you ever do.**

Invest the time today to teach the next generation. It will be one of the most rewarding things you ever do.

CHAPTER SUMMARY

- The leader selects, trains, and mentors the next generation of leaders.
- You are the chief talent scout, chief mentor, chief career counselor, and chief role model.
- Look for talent—that which you can neither learn nor teach, that predicts what you can do in the future.
- Once you have found talent, first convince the person they are talented.
- Talented people require career counseling, mentoring, and role modeling.
- Even as you start your journey of leadership, know that it will end.
- You must have a short- and long-term succession plan.
- You can learn as much from good bosses as from bad bosses. It's just more fun to learn from great leaders.
- No one is indispensable, including you.

For visual representation of this summary, see Figure 22.

WHAT AM I GOING TO DO DIFFERENTLY ON MONDAY?

- I will go through my roster of up-and-comers, pick three who I am going to mentor over the next year, and invite them individually to lunch or breakfast with me to start the process.
- I will schedule a meeting with my board in the next three to six months to discuss short- and long-term succession planning.
- I will find and join a professional mentoring organization.

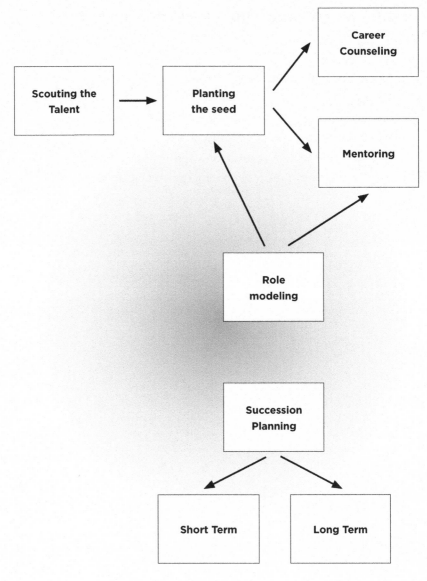

Figure 22

3

SECTION 3

CASE STUDIES

CASE STUDIES

Now that I've shown you the paradigm and discussed the seven non-delegable roles of the leader, it's time to put the model to work.

In the following chapters, I will present four case studies, hypothetical but based on actual events, of leaders using the seven non-delegables paradigm to solve four complex leadership problems.

I will present the scenario and the characters involved, and then show how the paradigm was used to address and resolve the fundamental problem facing that organization.

In the first example, the mandate for change is clear. Everyone is sensing the same thing: the barn is burning, and we must, together and quickly, put the fire out.

In the second example, only the leader recognizes that the barn is burning. No one else can tell (or they have their eyes firmly shut), and the leader's challenge is to help everyone see the need for systemic change and address it.

In the third example, I present a leader who is not adequately sensing that he needs to change, and therefore his boss has to help him recognize the issues and deal with them.

In the final example, the leader's boss does not understand and support the vision of the subordinate leader. The challenge is to bring the boss onboard with the vision plus the strategies to make the boss' and subordinate's models align.

Case Study #1
The Turnaround

11

The scenario

The Museum of Modern Art (MoMA) in a mid-sized New England city, a not-for-profit organization in existence for over a century, is bleeding members and money at an accelerating pace. The outgoing CEO, a beloved icon at the organization and in the city, has just retired after 23 years. The board of directors is deeply concerned about the negative membership and financial trends, and has decided to bring in an outsider to turn MoMA around.

The membership demographics have been changing rapidly. The "old guard" of aging wealthy donors is steadily disappearing. While young moneyed urban professionals are participating in MoMA activities, their contributions and memberships are not keeping up with vanishing older supporters.

The characters

The board selects Cynthia, a retired foreign service officer, as the new CEO. While she has a limited background in both membership and art, she is married to a classically trained art historian and spent years overseas in culturally rich environments. Post-retirement, Cynthia just finished a two-year consulting engagement with a membership organization, albeit not in the art world.

A highly experienced, dedicated, and stable staff has been in place for a long time, with an average tenure of more than 10 years.

The board is led by a progressive and aggressive local entrepreneur, who has been firing up board members with his insistence that change is necessary. Most, but not all, of the board is convinced.

Sensing

The new CEO spends the first three months, as well as her onboarding time, introducing herself and speaking to MoMA board and staff, members, potential members, stakeholders, and observers.

Her conversations focus on identifying MoMA's strengths, weaknesses, opportunities, and threats. She does a lot of listening.

Then she spends a week away from the office collating and integrating everything she had heard.

The hard and subjective data all say the same thing: quickly fix the major financial problems or MoMA is going out of business. It is not subtle!

MoMA has no formal strategic plan. Based on her consulting and leadership experience, Cynthia desperately wants to put in place a long-term vision and strategic plan for the organization. But it quickly becomes obvious that first she needs to stop the hemorrhaging of resources. She senses that while there is a place for formal vision and strategy, it is not going to be in the first two or three years.

She senses that while there is a place for formal vision and strategy, it is not going to be in the first two or three years.

In her conversations with existing and potential members and donors, she discerns that MoMA has little perceived relevance to potential new members, and older members have no desire to change. There is clear generational stress at MoMA.

In her conversations with staff, there is no sense of crisis and no desire to change. As far as MoMA staff are concerned, things are just fine.

Stakeholders and community leaders are oblivious to MoMA's problems. More troubling is the community's poor understanding and unwillingness to support MoMA's fundamental missions.

Visioning

Cynthia recognizes that she must do two things simultaneously, with two different audiences.

First, she has to focus the organization on the short-term actions and tactics necessary to staunch the financial bleeding.

Second, Cynthia recognizes that mere survival is not sufficient for long-term growth. While everyone else focuses on survival, she keeps thinking about what the long-term strategy and vision need to be. Using a firefighting metaphor, her team has to be fighting the fire, while she is thinking about how to prevent the next fire.

> **Using a firefighting metaphor, her team has to be fighting the fire, while she is thinking about how to prevent the next fire.**

The short-term solution becomes simple—stop the bleeding. And it isn't framed as a grand vision—just "stop the bleeding." Conventional thinking suggests that strategies should be long-term; however, in this case, the strategies all have two- to six-month time frames. Cynthia describes them as tactical strategies.

But Cynthia has more than an internal audience. She also needs to communicate with stakeholders, the community, and many younger potential members about the MoMA turnaround. In fact, Cynthia has two parallel sets of short-term strategies— one internal (stop the bleeding) and one external (MoMA is under new management, and we'd like you to support MoMA).

Acculturation

A proactive and innovative culture is required to turn MoMA around.

During her onboarding and in her initial interviews, Cynthia examines the toolset needed to survive in the short term and thrive in the long term. She divides her analysis into people, process, money, tools, priorities, and culture.

> **It quickly becomes obvious that the culture needs to completely change.**

It quickly becomes obvious that the culture needs to completely change— from a reactive to a proactive stance. Because it is a small organization, the issues of people and culture are very closely intertwined. It becomes clear that the veteran staff is not going to adapt to the new proactive culture. While everyone is given the opportunity to adopt the new culture, in the end the entire staff turns over in the next 18 months, and the roles of the staff members are completely reorganized.

The primary methodology for creating a new culture is hiring. Putting the right people in the right jobs—new staff who share Cynthia's passion, innovative spirit, and proactive philosophy— will go a long way toward turning the culture around.

But having new people on staff is not enough. Cynthia spends the first two years communicating, internally and externally, her message of a new MoMA. She uses the simplified model developed as part of the sensing process to give "elevator pitches" to stakeholders, members, potential members and key decision makers.

Enabling

Tools and money are also closely intertwined. The infrastructure of the organization is not suited to operating in a newer fast-paced and more technology-intensive environment.

The information technology is completely out of date. MoMA's Internet and social media presence are nonexistent.

The office spaces are dingy and run down. In fact, everywhere she looks, the infrastructure is failing.

Cynthia goes to the board and requests to dip into reserves to **Infrastructure is failing.**
completely replace the infrastructure. This is a difficult request, as reserves had been used to cover revenue shortfalls in previous years. She frames these new expenditures as existential necessities, and a nervous board approves them.

Drawing from reserves is not enough. Cynthia, with the advice of her artist husband, suggests the politically risky step of selling one or two works of art to raise the capital necessary to complete the infrastructure overall. While it takes a lot of convincing, eventually the board agrees to a private sale/lease-back agreement for one of the major works of art in the collection.

Cynthia and her staff examine MoMA's programs and services, and explicitly ask, "Is this program or service consistent with our direction?" With the concurrence of the board but with some grumbling from longtime board members, Cynthia eliminates two entrenched but high-cost/low-revenue programs.

Deciding

Initially it is Cynthia who makes almost all the decisions. She realizes that in the beginning, she has to be highly directive, because existing staff has neither the inclination nor the talent to make decisions that should properly have been delegated to them.

Delegation is minimal because the right people are not yet in position. Delegation is minimal because the right people are not yet in position.

After the first years, Cynthia embarks on a proactive plan to delegate more and more decisions to her newly hired and empowered staff. Cynthia does not want to use a top-down approach any longer than she needs to.

In the decision-making framework of chapter 8, Cynthia is initially operating in the chaotic mode—simply trying to restore order—knowing full well that she needs to get out of that mode as quickly as possible.

Responsibility

From day one, Cynthia publicly and privately accepts responsibility for all that happens. Cynthia uses the word "I" for the bad news and the word "we" (and usually the name of a specific member of the staff or board member) for the good news.

This is a real challenge in her relationships with the board, because Cynthia is the bearer of much bad news. For example, when she terminates several long-term beloved employees who could not adapt, she has to individually brief her board members about the "why" of the personnel changes.

> **The wave of bad news is part of turning MoMA around, and not a reflection of her competence.**

She has to educate the board that keeping them informed about everything is part of a new culture of transparency. The wave of bad news is part of turning MoMA around, and not a reflection of her competence.

Mentoring

In the first three years, there is a commitment to education—ensuring the new staff has the technical and operational skills necessary to be successful. There is little if any time spent on mentoring and succession planning.

> **As MoMA starts its turnaround, she implements both mentoring and succession planning.**

But Cynthia knows that mentoring and succession planning is critical to long-term success, so as soon as MoMA starts its turnaround, she implements both mentoring and succession planning for her team.

Key lessons

In a turnaround situation, the CEO must maintain a simultaneous short-term and long-term focus.

In the short term, the leader must stop the bleeding—turn the ship around or put out the fire. Pick your metaphor; the point is that the leader must fix the obvious problem(s).

But while everyone is scrambling, the leader must recognize that this phase is a relatively short-term phenomenon—so the leader must create a totally different organization that will succeed in the long run.

It is likely that the new CEO, to turn things around, will have to focus on changing the culture and replacing much of the infrastructure. This may require some gut-wrenching resource allocations and extremely difficult personnel decisions.

Change is hard. Strong support from the board combined with managing board expectations is critical to success because in the beginning the news will not be good—and the changes many and unpleasant.

Change is hard.

Case Study #2
The Tectonic
Shift

12

The scenario

The Palmyra Clinic is the leading obstetrics and gynecology (ObGyn) specialty group in a medium-sized Upper Midwest city about an hour from the state capital.

The clinic gradually grew from two married residency classmates in the early 1970s to now having 25 physicians. The clinic has been a fixture in the community for decades.

The overwhelming majority of births at the only local hospital are handled by clinic physicians.

The clinic elects one of their doctors as the CEO and hires a non-physician COO. The **Everyone is happy with the status quo.** physicians and staff are compensated generously, morale is excellent, and most everyone is happy with the status quo.

The clinic has seven-figure reserves, an excellent balance sheet, and has seen a steady increase in patient volume and revenue over the last decade.

Other than the physician CEO, the doctors are uninvolved in the running of the business and focus strictly on clinical care.

The characters

Megan, the elected physician CEO, has served superbly in her position for the past six years. She is technically and managerially competent, clinically respected, and well-liked by physicians and staff.

Stephan, the COO for the last three years, is also respected and well-liked by both physicians and staff. He has a well-deserved reputation for a deep understanding of the finances and business operations.

The situation has changed.

Over the past six quarters, Megan and Stephan have noticed a slow but accelerating erosion in the financials and patient demographics. Seasonally adjusted patient volume and revenue growth have slowed or gone negative.

> **Megan and Stephan have noticed a slow but accelerating erosion in the financials and patient demographics.**

The state's only academic medical center, located in the state capital, has begun to market aggressively within a hundred-mile radius. Billboards and marketing for their ObGyn services have cropped up everywhere. Innovative transportation programs are bringing patients to the academic medical center, eliminating the distance issue.

Megan and Stephan suspect that the long-standing and highly successful business model of the Palmyra Clinic may be in jeopardy.

> **Their role as leaders is first and foremost to determine whether an inflection point has truly occurred, or whether it's just a blip in the data.**

Their role as leaders is first and foremost to determine whether an inflection point has truly occurred, or whether it's just a blip in the data.

Sensing

Together, they gather additional data. They look at the demographics of their city, get into the details of the clinic financials, hire an outside consultant to assess the situation, and meet with fellow like-sized specialty medical group CEOs within the surrounding areas.

After a nine-month period of study and analysis, they determine that the problem is not internal to the clinic—the clinic is operating as efficiently as ever, if not more so.

They conclude that there are two problems.

First, the competition from the state's academic medical center is siphoning off high-end patients and revenue from the Palmyra Clinic and other single-specialty ObGyn groups within a hundred-mile radius of the state capital.

Second, coincident with increased competition, the emergence of the Affordable Care Act significantly changed the patient and revenue mix. The Palmyra Clinic is seeing many more previously uninsured patients with lower compensation while simultaneously losing high-end patients. The ground under their feet has shifted.

Using the precepts of chapter 4, Megan and Stephan extrapolate the data. The future does not look good.

Using the principles of Kuhn's paradigm shifts and Christensen's disruptive process change, it becomes painfully obvious that the clinic needs to fundamentally change.

The data clearly indicates an inflection point, and the inflection point is rooted in changes to the paradigm and the processes.

> **The data clearly indicates an inflection point, and the inflection point is rooted in changes to the paradigm and the processes.**

Absent systemic change, sooner or later, the clinic will fail.

Visioning

It is clear to the leader and her principal deputy, but no one else in leadership, that their decades-long business model is unsustainable and will likely fail. The physicians and staff of the clinic are oblivious to the changes, as they are focused on clinical care and optimizing the operation of the clinic.

The clinic needs a new vision and a new strategic plan.

The clinic needs a new vision and a new strategic plan.

Megan and Stephan together must guide the physicians and senior staff to a new plan, with attendant changes in the vision, strategies, tools, and culture of the organization.

Megan and Stephan lead a very difficult offsite that highlights the new reality to physicians and senior staff. The data, once contextualized, is very clear, and the conclusions are unavoidable. And the physicians and senior staff are not happy. But, in the vernacular, it's either change or die.

The simple yet powerful mission created by the founding pair of physicians, "The Palmyra Clinic provides the best Ob/Gyn service in our city," does not change. The physicians and staff are committed to it.

The vision and strategies to meet the mission of the clinic absolutely must change.

The leadership team develops a new vision and strategies emphasizing the long-term relationship between the clinic and its patients, the clinic's proximity to the patients, and the clinic's high-end technology. The new vision addresses why patients do not need to travel to the state capital when they can get superlative care here, today, at the clinic, from their local doctors and staff. After all, who really cares about you if not your neighbor?

Acculturation

The most difficult change will be to the culture.

The physicians and staff have been comfortable and well

off for decades. The new vision and strategies caused by the changing environment will take many physicians and staff out of their comfort zone, causing disruptions and difficulties.

This is where Megan's biggest challenge lies. She will have to proselytize individually and collectively for a new culture. She will

> **The most difficult change will be to change the culture.**

have to make sure of her support from fellow physicians while simultaneously motivating them to change. Most difficult of all, she will have to make tough personnel decisions, particularly about senior staff and long serving physicians who are unwilling or unable to change.

Her most important asset will be the unwavering support of Stephan. He will need to educate and motivate the staff. While the doctors (mostly) believe Megan, they will certainly come to him privately, as the business wizard, and ask, "Is it really that bad that we have to change this dramatically?" There can be no daylight between Megan and Stephan.

Enabling

The clinic, for the last ten years, has run extremely efficiently and effectively. The current tools are optimized for the current paradigm.

> **New vision and strategies will require different tools.**

But the new vision and strategies may require different tools.

Megan and Stephan need to make sure that they have the right tools. They hire a consultant to do a complete review of systems to make sure that the current tools are more than adequate for the new vision and strategies. They look at people, process, money, hardware, priorities, and knowledge.

While a seven-figure reserve would ideally remain untouched, the clinic will need to draw down some of the

> **Change will not come cheap!**

reserves to provide the money necessary to change—whether it's for purchasing new

IT systems, adding high-end technology, hiring people with new and different skills, or investing in additional training.

Change will not come cheap!

Deciding

The decision-making process for the CEO will be much more difficult during this time of change.

On the one hand, Megan must be directive and firm—there

> **Megan must be tactically impatient.**

is a clear and present danger to the clinic. She must be tactically impatient.

On the other hand, Megan and Stephan need to employ the complex decision-making process, discussed in chapter 8, on many issues, where all of the answers and indeed many of the questions are not yet necessarily known. She must be strategically patient.

Megan's decision-making must be very nuanced, and her process for making decisions will require explanation and buy-in from her fellow physicians. She must proceed very thoughtfully to make sure she does not lose the trust of her fellow physicians.

> **She must be strategically patient.**

Constant communication and total transparency are the keys to success.

Responsibility

This will be a difficult and very stressful time for Megan. She will feel the weight of responsibility for the survival of the clinic on her shoulders.

While not micromanaging, she has to stay totally focused on the long-term health of the clinic and accept that it is her responsibility and hers alone to make the transition a success, while still delegating authority to those who must make changes.

She should reach out to other single-specialty clinics in the state to form a support group.

She should find a mentor who has undergone a similar transition and perhaps even hire a personal coach.

And she must go out of her way to deepen the relationship between herself and Stephan—the two of them must be absolutely synchronized.

And Megan must take of herself and her relationship with her spouse. For so many reasons, she cannot afford to crash physically or emotionally.

Mentoring

Mentoring the next generation and ensuring succession planning will become incredibly important during this time of deep cultural change.

A whole new generation of clinic physician leaders will have to be educated and motivated, since the previous generation will quickly see that their roles in the new schema will have changed to the point where they may not want to participate anymore.

Megan needs to look for a long-term successor who will carry the change forward at some future point.

Key lessons

In stable, successful organizations, it is often only the leader who first senses the potential tectonic shifts in the environment for the organization.

Once she senses that the model has changed, the leader, often lonely because everyone else just wants to keep on doing what they've been doing, must bring the guiding coalition together to create the sense of urgency that allows the problem to be addressed.

In many cases, radical shifts in the tools (people, process, money, hardware, procedures, priorities, and culture) are required.

The leader must acknowledge and adapt to the stress and personal challenges of leading in a time of crisis. She needs to reach out for as much help and support as possible.

The leader must balance the exigent necessities of chaotic decision-making with the patience associated with complex decision-making.

A whole new generation of leaders will have to be identified and groomed for the new reality.

Case Study #3 Explosive Growth

13

The characters

For 25 years, Carl has been dedicated to the mission of music education for disadvantaged kids.

After graduating from the conservatory in a major Northwest city, Carl created a not-for-profit, KidsMusic, whose mission was to provide instrumental and vocal enrichment for kids in the poorest neighborhoods of his hometown. KidsMusic teaches afterschool vocal and instrumental music to more than a thousand kids every year.

Starting with $300 and no staff, Carl created a not-for-profit organization that now has a staff of 10 and a budget of $2.2 million.

Carl is a charismatic and highly regarded entrepreneur. He is recognized as one of the most effective fundraisers in the city. Every year, donor dollars continue to increase.

He works 60 hours per week raising money and gives all outward appearance of burnout.

While he has delegated the program operations to two very talented recent graduates of a local MBA program, he is still involved in many decisions that could easily be construed as micromanagement.

His board has recently expanded by adding more seasoned business executives and high-net-worth individuals. Angela, the board chair, is the regional VP of one of the largest banks in the West.

Everyone associated with KidsMusic, on the staff, and on the board is passionately positive and incredibly enthusiastic about the mission of bringing music education to those who would never otherwise receive it.

The scenario

After 18 months as the board chair, Angela, an experienced executive, senses that KidsMusic is a classic case of an organization growing beyond the skill set of its founder.

Angela has gently had the conversation with Carl that perhaps it's time to bring on a more experienced executive as CEO while allowing Carl time to focus on what he loves to do—fundraising and proselytizing. Carl is not responsive to that line of thinking.

Carl frequently complains that he is working too hard and that he is underpaid. He adamantly resists any suggestion to change the current organizational structure. While strongly supportive of his two young deputies, he refuses to delegate any decision-making.

The sophisticated board is becoming more and more concerned about Carl's unwillingness to adapt to the changing organization. At the same time, the board recognizes that Carl is the charismatic face of KidsMusic, and unilaterally removing him from the picture would create existential problems for the organization.

Sensing

The objective data is generally positive. However, a deeper dive into revenue and expense data shows that without any reserves to buffer cash-flow variations, KidsMusic has several times come perilously close to not meeting payroll. In addition, Carl has committed to expanding several programs without ensuring downstream cash flows.

The subjective data is less sanguine. The tension between Carl and the board, particularly the more experienced executives on the board, has slowly ratcheted up. Carl is leery of any new direction, yet several of his personnel and organizational decisions have put KidsMusic potentially at risk.

Everyone on the board realizes that an inflection point has already been reached.

Everyone on the board realizes that an inflection point has already been reached.

In this case study, the CEO is not fulfilling one of his major roles—to be the chief sensor! He is blind to the fact that KidsMusic is growing so rapidly that the leadership model for the organization is not capable of effectively managing the growth.

What got Carl and KidsMusic here will not get KidsMusic there – in fact, operating in the past has the potential to destroy KidsMusic.

Visioning

Everyone, including Carl, realizes that the organization needs a new vision as it transitions from an exponential-growth start-up to a steady-growth sustainable organization.

With Carl and his senior staff, the board creates a new vision and attendant strategies that would make KidsMusic to a successful and sustainable growing organization. Over Carl's active and passive objections, one of the strategies is written to develop a leadership model that would support the new reality of a sustainably growing organization. After all, Carl says in private and public, things are just fine!

Enabling

This is a case where the only tool that needs to be changed is the CEO. If Carl, after extensive coaching and advice, is still unable or unwilling to change, then it's time for the board to change the CEO.

> **The only tool that needs to be changed is the CEO.**

This is much easier said than done, given Carl's reputation and ability to bring in money.

It now falls to the board to enable the vision by creating a transition that is neither disruptive nor ineffective.

Acculturation

Culture almost always starts at the top. However, this is one of those rare situations where the culture has evolved from below. Everyone in the organization has shifted from entrepreneurial to sustaining—except the boss.

This is a much greater challenge than it seems, because the leader has not accepted that it is the leader who needs to change. This is the most difficult of all culture changes.

Regretfully, when the leader is stuck in a culture that doesn't work and does not adapt, the board must change the leader.

Deciding and Responsibility

Decision-making processes that work for a start-up are rarely effective for a sustaining organization.

Carl must change his decision-making by delegating both the decision-making and the attendant authority. This is a challenge for someone who has made almost every decision for a quarter century.

The unfortunate possibility is that the leader doesn't change, decision-making does not get delegated to the right level, and the organization slowly withers because decisions are made at the wrong level or not made at all.

Mentoring

It is now the board's responsibility to mentor Carl and to ensure a transition plan exists, as there is a real possibility that the CEO will not be able to adapt and change.

The board directs Carl to find a personal coach who he is comfortable with. While Carl objects that he doesn't need or want a trainer, the board is adamant. And the board adds two important caveats to the contract with the coach—the board chair will meet one-one with the personal coach prior to finalizing the contract, and will meet monthly with Carl and the coach together to go over progress and plans.

The board will receive joint quarterly reports from the board chair and the coach.

Key lessons

For the MoMA, the need for change was obvious to everyone. A new leader was brought in with a mandate for change.

For the Palmyra Clinic, the need for change first became apparent to the leader, and she quickly rallied the organization to change.

In the KidsMusic example, the leader was unwilling or unable to see the need for change. The leader was the problem.

When the leader is the problem, it makes the challenge much greater.

The leader must be coached and offered help, but the mandate to change the leader's behavior must be forceful. And the board needs to think through, in private, the various departure contingencies.

Case Study #4
My boss won't sing along!!

14

The scenario & the characters

James is the physician head of one of three geographically dispersed branch clinics for a rural community hospital system in southwestern Colorado. After completing medical school and residency, James returned to practice medicine in the small city in which he was born and raised. Over the last two years, he obtained an Executive MBA from the local state university.

He reports to Annamarie, the head of the community hospital system. She has been with the hospital system for more than 30 years and is a community icon. She was the first female physician to practice orthopedics in this rural part of the state.

The community hospital system has been under financial pressure since the inception of the Affordable Care Act. They are taking care of more, sicker, and more poorly reimbursed patients than ever before. At the same time, they're having trouble recruiting physicians and staff, given the relatively low pay scale in rural community clinics.

James, over the last five years, has introduced many radical innovations in his branch clinic. Following a detailed analysis of the financial and operational situation, he implemented strategies based on a vision of making the branch clinic financially viable while providing superlative medical quality. He has been wildly successful, and his branch clinic's achievements were recently featured in a national TV show.

But he's hitting two walls. First, he needs more capital to make the next flight of improvements. Second, his two branch clinic counterparts, who are not doing nearly as well, have soured Annamarie against many of the improvements he has made and wants to make.

Sensing

James has done a superlative job of sensing, visioning, and creating strategies for improvement *within* the branch clinic.

But he has not brought his boss, and the parent organization, onboard. They don't really understand what he has done and why, and they tepidly support his model, his vision, and his strategies. In fact, he knows that the other two branch clinics are envious of his success, and he suspects that Annamarie is becoming fearful of being replaced.

> **But he has not brought his boss, and the parent organization, onboard.**

He must incorporate the needs and issues of the parent organization into his model.

The "what's in it for me" for Annamarie and the community hospital system is not clear. This situation is almost the exact opposite of the KidsMusic case, where the CEO of the rapidly growing organization had done little if any sensing, visioning, and strategizing. In the KidsMusic example, it was Carl's boss, his board chair, who had to force him to do the sensing, visioning, and strategizing he needed to do. In this case, it's James's boss and his peers who need to come onboard.

Visioning

James needs to proceed on two parallel paths.

First, his vision must expand so it incorporates the needs of the parent community hospital system with the terrific work he's already done at the branch clinic. Essentially, he must create a "what's in it for the community hospital *system*."

Second, he needs to change his approach to Annamarie so that in his communication with her he focuses on "what's in it for *her*." When he asks for additional resources, it's not to make his branch clinic function better, but rather to make the community hospital system work better.

Enabling

In this example, it is the need to expand James's toolset—acquire more resources—that is driving the need to change the vision. Unlike in other examples where the vision drives the tools, in this case, it is the tools (really, the lack thereof) that drive the vision.

Acculturation

Just as James needs to change his modus operandi vis-à-vis the community hospital system, his team needs to take a much more collective approach to working with the other branch clinics.

And just as James is working hard to help Annamarie, the culture on James's team needs to change. James's team needs to shift from competition to cooperation. "What can we do to help you? What can we do for you to make your life easier?" should be two questions constantly asked and answered to their counterparts in the other clinics, and to the parent. That's a significant change in culture, but without that change, James will not get far.

James needs to clearly promulgate, proselytize, and enforce a culture of "we the community hospital system" as opposed to "we the branch clinic."

Responsibility

James's approach needs to be that he is responsible for more than just his branch clinic. If he takes a more holistic approach, taking responsibility for the system instead of his branch clinic, that will translate to more cooperation from Annamarie.

Mentoring

Normally, we think about mentoring as from a senior to a junior. In this case, James may want to think about peer mentoring his two less effective clinic heads. While it may be challenging in the beginning, if he is tactful and humble, he might convert competitors into allies by showing them how to be more successful.

Key lessons

Leadership often involves leading your peers and leading your bosses.

Leading up is a cultural change for both the leader and his team. Sometimes you need to mentor your peers.

SUMMARY & AFTERWORD

This book is about defining a process, a model, a paradigm, a way of thinking, for and about leadership.

If you don't have a model, a paradigm, a meta-process for leadership, you're doing improv leadership—sometimes entertaining, but fundamentally unguided. And improv leadership is scary for everyone you lead and everyone who wants you to be successful.

So you need a paradigm for how you are going to lead, just like you need a plan to accomplish a project.

The paradigm I developed for myself and have now shared with you is to *focus first and foremost on deciding what is so important, so critical, so difficult, that only you, the boss, can successfully accomplish it – the seven non-delegables.*

Articulate first those things that you are not going to delegate, and then you have defined those things that you are going to do that matter.

Be the Chief Sensor, the Chief Visionary, the Chief Culture Officer, the Chief Enabler, the Chief Decider, and the Chief Mentor, and Embrace being Responsible for it all.

Everything else is delegated to your team.

I have tried to shift the conversation from delegating as little as possible and assuming responsibility for little, to assuming responsibility for everything and delegating as much as possible.

In the middle of my professional life, I heard a truism that has been incredibly helpful: "10 percent of effective leadership is knowing the right answer, and 90 percent of effective leadership is knowing the *right question(s) to ask, and the wrong answer(s)."*

I want my doctor to know the right answer close to always, not just 10 percent of the time. But I'm not paying my doctor to be a leader, I'm paying her to be an expert, so the 10 percent—90 percent rule is not applicable to expertise.

The 10 percent—90 percent rule for leadership takes away much of the onus on the leader having technical expertise and replaces it with an emphasis on understanding what matters—knowing by training, instinct, or experience what is right—and what is wrong.

If you know the right question(s) to ask, and if you know, based on experience, training, instinct, or this book, that the answer(s) is/are wrong, then you can guide your team to the right answer.

I hope that this book has given you some perspectives and ideas, so that when you and your team are considering answers that don't feel right, you can say, *"Let's think about that a little bit more. I remember this book I read about the seven non-delegables of the leader—let's talk with those in mind."*

If you reach for this book or you remember some of what I have shared, then I will have been successful.

I wrote this book to make a difference in the lives of those who have taken on the difficult and rewarding mantle of leadership. Good luck and Godspeed.

—Tom Gehring
San Diego, Summer 2018

ACKNOWLEDGMENTS

I want to start by first acknowledging my wife of 35 years, partner for 40 years, and friend of 44 years, Catherine Moore, MD. A practicing psychiatrist for a third of a century, she has taught me so much about myself and the human mind.

Many have contributed to the making of the book. I want to recognize the readers of the first draft—Matthew Amsden, James and Carmen Beaubeaux, Leslie Bruce, Jeff Fischbeck, Bob Freund, Jim Hay, John Krause, David Oates, Deirdre Maloney, Peter MacCracken, and Rob Pennoyer.

There were many who read subsequent drafts, but I want to express my special thanks to Claude Barron, Dan Chavez, Jeremy Dendle, Bob Durham, Beth Howell, Charlie Martoglio, Mark Moore, and Joel Roos for their insightful and honest comments.

My hat is off to Deirdre Maloney for being my first mentor in the two-year process of writing this book. At each step of the way, she was generous with her time and ideas.

I want to recognize everyone in the past decade with whom I've discussed the non-delegables and who helped me grow them from a fuzzy pretty-good idea to a mature paradigm. In particular, my appreciation to Bob Freund for helping me think through and verbalize the last of the seven!

I want to thank Robin Samora and her husband Steve who provided the impetus to write the book. Over an evening fire in upstate New Hampshire in 2016, she and her husband - having never met me, independently and with nothing to gain or lose – provided the final impetus for me to sit down and write the book.

My thanks to my second mentor, Karla Olson, who guided me through the process of getting a first-time author's manuscript to print. The fabulous design team of Alan Dino Hebel and Ian Koviak at *the*BookDesigners made my words look great.

And finally, my thanks to my son and my father, my greatest teachers.

BIBLIOGRAPHY

- John Kotter, *Leading Change*
- David Marquette, *Turn the Ship Around*
- Marcus Buckingham, *First, Break All the Rules*
- Thomas Kuhn, *The Theory of Scientific Revolutions*
- Clayton Christensen, *The Innovator's Dilemma*
- Joseph L. Bower & Clayton M. Christensen, *Disruptive Technologies: Catching the Wave, Harvard Business Review,* January 1995.
- Dave Logan, *Tribal Leadership*
- David Snowden & Mary Boone, "A Leader's Framework for Decision-Making," *Harvard Business Review,* November 2007.
- Scott Adams, *Dogbert's Top-Secret Management Handbook*
- Patrick Lencioni, *The Advantage*
- Simon Sinek, *Start With Why*

BIOGRAPHY

Tom Gehring was born in Cologne, Germany in 1953, and lived in Germany, France, India and the United States before graduating from Rice University with a double major in Electrical Engineering and Applied Mathematics in 1976.

He served for 22 years in the United States Navy, almost all of it at sea in submarines.

After retiring from active duty in 1998, he spent three years at Booz|Allen|Hamilton as a senior strategic consultant.

From 2001 until his retirement in 2015 he was the CEO of the San Diego County Medical Society (SDCMS), representing more than 8,000 physicians in the eighth-largest city in the United States.

APPENDIX 1: PRETTY GOOD RULES & QUESTIONS FOR LEADERS

- KISS—keep it simple and short.
- Nothing hard is ever easy.
- Knowing the right thing to do is easy. Doing the right thing is hard. —*General Norman Schwarzkopf*
- Why? Why? Why? Why? Why? Why? —*Admiral Hyman Rickover*
- You lead from the front. —*my father, Ted Gehring*
- Ninety percent of effective leadership is knowing the right question to ask—and the wrong answer.
- No one ever talked a ship to sea—you gotta' do stuff to get underway.
- Improvise, adapt, and overcome. —*actor Clint Eastwood in the movie* Heartbreak Ridge
- What are you going to do differently on Monday?
- You can't fix what ain't broke—but you can watch it very carefully.
- Life is tough but is tougher if you're stupid. —*actor John Wayne in the movie* The Sands of Iwo Jima
- You can't fix stupid.

- You do what you can, where you're at, with what you have. — *President Theodore Roosevelt*
- Don't stop in the middle of the freeway.
- No plan ever survives first contact with the enemy or with reality.
- Good judgment comes from experience, and experience comes from bad judgment.
- The buck stops here. —*President Harry Truman*
- If in a tough spot, ask out loud, in public, "What's the right thing to do here?"
- In a tough spot, ask out loud, in public, "Is this legal, ethical, and moral?"
- Never argue with an idiot in public—you won't win, and those watching won't be able to tell the difference between you and the idiot.
- What just didn't happen here?
- Plans are nothing, planning is everything. —*General Dwight D. Eisenhower.*

APPENDIX 2: ONE CEO'S LEADERSHIP PHILOSOPHY

Below is a *verbatim* transcript of the philosophy statement that hung over my desk during my time as CEO. It was a living document that I periodically revised and reissued. Every member of my team had the document, as did my bosses. Since I plagiarized shamelessly to create this document, please do not hesitate to use it for whatever helps you become a better leader.

Eagle-eyed proofreaders amongst you will notice there is a typo: "monthly" is *deliberately* misspelled. I wanted to quickly teach my team that I was not infallible, and that I expected, demanded in fact, that they correct me when I was wrong.

So if, after first reading it, they did not come back to me with a correction, I used that as a teachable moment – for better proofreading if they didn't catch the mistake, and for the expectation of that they correct me if I was wrong if they caught it and didn't mention it.

I'm a hard charger and a pragmatist—I expect you to be the same.

The physicians define a job well done.

We exist, as an organization and as employees, to serve our member Physicians.

Anticipate and deliver what Physician members of SDCMS consider value.

If SDCMS does not satisfy the requirements of physician members, someone else will.

Process, Output and Outcome

Use a process driven approach to problem solving.

Document, understand, and improve your processes.

Initiate planned abandonment regularly.

Hate bureaucracy—challenge rules or processes that slow execution or fail to add value.

Communicating

"I don't know" is an acceptable answer.

If you don't understand, ask.

If you're mad at me, or when (not if) I'm wrong, tell me.

Keep the written and spoken word short and to the point.

When we talk, give me the short version first. Insist on giving me the long version if you feel it necessary.

When you write, use the format "Facts, Discussion, Action".

- Facts = what do you know.
- Discussion = what do you think.
- Action = what do you want (me) to do.

When you give a presentation, answer the following questions for the person receiving the brief:

- What do you want them to do?
- Why do you want the them to do that?
- What's in it for the them?
- How much does it cost and how long will it take?

Always feel free to call me—anytime, anywhere, for any reason. If in doubt about calling, call. If in doubt about being in doubt, call.

Mistakes & Risk

Take risks—but understand the risk, bound the risk and keep me cut in.

I do not tolerate unmitigated risks, errors or omissions on items identified as "Mission Critical."

Mistakes happen—tell me about them.

Identify and fix the root cause of mistakes.

Honesty

Tell the truth—always—above all, to yourself.

Do the right thing. If it feels wrong, it probably is.

There are no secrets.

Keep your promises.

I expect candor—if "the emperor has no clothes", say so.

Assignments

If I want you to drop everything, I will tell you.

Discuss our collective focus/issues/agendas/approach prior to proceeding.

Keep me posted. Let me know when you will complete assignments and stick to your deadlines.

Keep a list of your pending work for me.

Keep a PUBLIC list of your top 10 focus points. Share them with me montlhy.

Know your focus. Keep the focus in focus.

Interactions

When communicating with other organizations, the word "No" belongs to me unless the request is illegal, unethical or immoral.

Never get into an argument (as opposed to a discussion)

with a physician or an organization unless I know about it.

If anyone behaves inappropriately with you, tell me immediately.

Feedback

We will meet for at least one hour every quarter to talk about us. Please take responsibility for making that happen.

I will provide you written feedback annually. I will ask the staff to do likewise for me.

Meetings

I hate long meetings.

Meetings will start and end on time. If you must be late, please let me know ahead of time.

If you are not ready for a meeting, reschedule the meeting and get ready.

Send me a post-meeting e-mail on all commitments made.

Network

We are a network, not a hierarchy.

Communicate, communicate, communicate and communicate again.

Serve each other's needs—we are a team.

Technology

I want us to be on the cutting edge of new technology as soon as possible.

Technology is a servant, not a master.

Passion

See change as opportunity, not threat.

Believe you can change the world.

If in doubt, the glass is half-full!

INDEX

Made in the USA
Coppell, TX
31 August 2020

35244531R00125